Ken's book is a fantastic read that serves to remind us that the God of the Bible is still alive and active in the world today. Not only does God offer us the joy of salvation and forgiveness through the substitutionary atonement of Christ on the Cross—he offers us life to the fullest! You will read of modern-day miracles, the joy of lives redeemed, the power of prayer, and the importance of obedience. If you've ever wondered what kind of miracles God is doing today, this book is a must read. If you've wondered what it means to live a life of dependence on Christ, this book is an 'everyman's' guide to pursuing God. Written with simple clarity and dependence on the word of God, this book will guide you into more fully pursuing the life God has called every believer to live.

Mike Picconatto
Pastor
Staples Alliance Church

Ken Peterson has combined the truths of scripture with his own personal experiences into a heartfelt testimony of this walk of faith. Ken has great examples of God's fingerprints all over his life, and he shares how God's plan of salvation was revealed to him. This book echoes what has been written in the scriptures as Ken gives its readers a better understanding of a wide variety of topics, from 'Seeking God' to the 'Power of Prayer.'

Patrick Humphrey
Student of the Bible, Teacher

But they that wait upon the LORD shall renew their strength; they shall mount up with wings as eagles; they shall run, and not be weary; and they shall walk, and not faint.

(Isaiah 40:31, KJV)

a walk with God

Jennifer,

May God bless you always.

Ken

Ken Peterson

a walk with God
one man's journey of faith

Tate Publishing & *Enterprises*

A Walk with God
Copyright © 2008 by Ken Peterson. All rights reserved.

No part of this publication may be reproduced, stored in a retrieval system or transmitted in any way by any means, electronic, mechanical, photocopy, recording or otherwise without the prior permission of the author except as provided by USA copyright law.

Scripture quotations marked "NLT" are taken from the *Holy Bible, New Living Translation,* Copyright © 1996. Used by permission of Tyndale House Publishers, Inc. All rights reserved.

The opinions expressed by the author are not necessarily those of Tate Publishing, LLC.

Published by Tate Publishing & Enterprises, LLC
127 E. Trade Center Terrace | Mustang, Oklahoma 73064 USA
1.888.361.9473 | www.tatepublishing.com

Tate Publishing is committed to excellence in the publishing industry. The company reflects the philosophy established by the founders, based on Psalm 68:11,
"The Lord gave the word and great was the company of those who published it."

Book design copyright © 2008 by Tate Publishing, LLC. All rights reserved.
Cover & Interior design by Kellie Southerland

Published in the United States of America

ISBN: 978-1-60799-110-6
1. Autobiography   2. Personal Memoirs
09.03.25

Dedication

I dedicate this book to God the Father, His Son, Jesus Christ, and to the Holy Spirit who dwells within me. It is God who inspired me to write this; He loves me and gave Himself for me, and I love Him in return.

To my wife, Julie, who has stood by me through everything, I cannot express in words the gratitude I feel, or the love that I have for you.

To my children, Matthew, Kayla, and Jared, who sacrificed time they could have spent with their dad, so that I could study God's Word, teach it to others and write this book. I love you guys with all my heart!

To all Christians everywhere—I pray that you will grow in your faith and draw closer to God because of what He has revealed to me and written through me in these pages.

I also dedicate this book to "The Lost" (those who do not know God). I pray that you will find your way to Him by what you read here.

When I put God first in my life, He did an amazing thing. He gave me a huge heart with a tremendous capacity to love all people, and because of that I love all of you; this book is for you!

Acknowledgments

I could not have written this book without the biblical references that I received from *Bible Gateway*. It is a magnificent search-tool for scripture.

To the translators of the New Living Translation Bible: I really appreciate the ease of understanding scripture that this translation has given to me.

I wish to thank all of the people at Tate Publishing for believing in me, for helping me through this process and for making this dream come true.

I would also like to thank Hannah Landecker for her contribution to this book, by writing about her faith experience and allowing me to include it.

To my wife and children, thanks for supporting me in this venture.

Last but not least, thank you to all the people who prayed for me during this endeavor.

Contents

- *15* Introduction
- *19* How I Became a Christian
- *49* By Faith
- *71* Obedience
- *99* Knowing God
- *127* Seeking God
- *141* The Power of Prayer
- *159* God's Call to Persevere

Introduction

I would like to start out by introducing who I am. I want you to know that I am not anyone special. I don't have a degree in ministry, nor have I had any formal Bible training. I'm really not even a writer, but I am writing this book in obedience to God.

I am simply a follower of Jesus Christ. I am a sinner who has been redeemed by "The blood of the Lamb."

Ever since I became a born-again Christian, in February of 1999, my life has not been the same. God has given me an intense desire to seek His face, to know His will and to search for Truth.

I have been reading and studying The Bible ever since. God has revealed much to me as I seek Him. He has revealed Himself to me through His Word, and through multiple encounters with God that I have experienced as I walk daily with Him.

I have always felt a need to write about these experiences, so that I can keep a permanent record of these events. I know how easily that I can forget the details of these experiences if I don't do this. I think about how God asked the

Israelites to take stones from the Jordan River, after God stopped the flow of the river, so that "His chosen people" could cross into the "Promised Land" on dry ground, and He had them pile the stones near the riverbank as a memorial to this event (Joshua 4).

With each encounter, I find that God teaches me new lessons and reveals new insights about Himself and His ways. I have been collecting these stories for a number of years, and now I feel that God wants me to share these experiences and lessons with others.

I believe that by sharing our experiences with each other, we can all learn from one another and grow to know God better. I don't believe that God reveals all things to one individual, but that He reveals parts to everyone. God does it this way so that we will remain dependant on Him and dependant on each other.

The Apostle Paul wrote, "Now we see things imperfectly as in a poor mirror, but then we will see everything with perfect clarity. All that I know now is partial and incomplete, but then I will know everything completely, just as God knows me now" (1 Corinthians 13:12, NLT).

God continues to reveal new things to me each day. I want you to know that this book is only about what I know to this point. It is not complete. It is only a small glimpse of the realities of God.

I don't write this book to boast about myself, or my experiences with God. But my hope is that by reading about my experiences and the things that God has revealed to me, that your own faith in God may grow and that you may be able to trust Him more and know Him better.

God wants a personal, and unique relationship with each one of us. It is His desire that all people would be saved, and that none of us would perish (2 Peter 3:9).

"For I take no pleasure in the death of anyone, declares the Sovereign LORD. Repent and live!" (Ezekiel 18:32, NIV).

But God will not force Himself into our life. God has given us free will to choose for ourselves if we want to be with God, or forever be separated from Him.

I pray that you will choose to believe in Him, to trust Him, and to follow Him.

I start this book with my own personal testimony of how I came to accept Jesus Christ as my LORD and Savior. But again, I do not write this to boast about myself, but to boast about how God can take a sinner like me, and transform them into a new creation if we allow Him to.

I share this with you, so that if you don't know Jesus Christ as your personal LORD and Savior you may be able to find your way to Christ through reading about how it happened for me. However, you cannot follow someone else's exact footsteps, it will be different and unique for each person.

As you read this book you will find that I use scriptures often. This is because I believe that God's words are much more meaningful and are able to make so much more impact than my own words could ever do. "For the word of God is living and active. Sharper than any double-edged sword, it penetrates even to dividing soul and spirit, joints and marrow; it judges the thoughts and attitudes of the heart" (Hebrews 4:12, NIV).

With that, I hope that you enjoy this book; may God bless you as you read it!

In Christ's Love,

Ken

How I Became A Christian

I was born November 18, 1959, the third child in a family of eventually seven children. I was baptized into the Roman Catholic Church a few days later. I was raised in the Catholic faith, receiving first communion at age seven, and being confirmed about six years later. I felt full of the Holy Spirit on the day I was confirmed, but my Christian journey did not end there.

My faith took a turn for the worse when I was only sixteen-years old.

It started because I had broken my arm several times by then, and each time it was my right arm. This happened every third year since I'd started school. In first grade, a classmate pushed me as I was swinging on the monkey bars. I fell and cracked my collarbone. In fourth grade, I fell on the ice and cracked my collarbone again. In seventh grade I cracked three bones in my right hand when the crank on the hoist of a grain-wagon slipped from my hand and came around and smacked me on top of it.

Now I was about to start tenth grade and this would be the year for breaking my right arm again (if the pattern of every third year continued). I was beginning football practice soon, and I feared it would happen while playing football. So, I prayed every night for a month that I would not break my right arm. I didn't care if I was even on the starting team, I just did not want to end up with a broken arm again.

On the first day of school it happened; I was tackling a guy, and another player came in headfirst and smashed my elbow between his helmet and the shoulder pads of the other player. My elbow was crushed. It took over a year and a half to recover the use of my arm; it still bothers me every day and will not straighten.

I felt God had let me down, and that He didn't care about me and He certainly does not answer prayers. I even doubted that He was real. I thought, *Surely this was not too much to ask for. How could I be anymore specific than, "Please, don't let me break my right arm?"*

About this same time, I started drinking. I didn't know exactly why: if it was for fun, or to fill a void left inside of me, or to numb the pain. But I know that I used alcohol to drown out the Spirit of God in me. I didn't want to hear that voice inside of me that tells me right from wrong. Soon it started to fade away; it was still there, I just couldn't hear it anymore.

I dreamed of becoming a pilot since I was 12-years old when I first saw an airplane spraying the neighbor's field. I began to turn that dream into reality by taking flying lessons as a senior in high school, and in the summer after graduation, I received my private pilot's license. It was an exhilarating experience to be at the controls of an airplane as the sole occupant.

I continued studying the art of flying in college, majoring in Agricultural Aviation. I worked hard those years, with a full time job, besides taking extra credits beyond a full schedule of classes. Flight lessons were expensive, and I was trying to pay my own way through college.

That first year of college would be the third year once again in the breaking-my–right arm-every-third-year curse. I didn't take any chances at all, or do anything that might possibly risk breaking my arm during that entire year. This time I was determined to take it into my own hands to ensure that I would not break my arm again, and break the three-year cycle. I succeeded, and began relying more on my-self rather than on God.

I graduated from college with an Associate in Applied Science degree in Agricultural Aviation, a commercial pilot license and a flight instructor certificate.

I sent out two hundred resumes to businesses located in Minnesota, and got one job offer. It was from Benson Flying Service in Benson, Minnesota. My job responsibilities included flight instructing, flying chartered flights for area businesses, and aerial photography. The company was also doing aerial spraying with two airplanes and three helicopters. This was the part that interested me most, and before the end of that first summer I was piloting one of the spray planes across the fields of west-central Minnesota.

I was still praying and going to church, and trying to rebuild my relationship with God, but with little faith. Although, I did pray for God to find me the perfect mate, and to make sure that I would know the one when she came along. This is one prayer that He did answer. While I was living in Benson, I met my wife, Julie. We fell instantly in love and got married several months later.

Life was going along fairly well, except that I was drinking heavily every night and I wasn't getting along with my boss. I started looking for another job when I heard that his son was moving back to work in the company; I knew that there wouldn't be room for me anymore. I found a job twenty miles away in Morris, Minnesota. I had just accepted the job, and before giving notice, I received a letter from Benson Flying Service saying exactly what I had feared: that they would not be employing me in the following year. I was relieved to have another job already lined up.

We bought a fixer-upper house in Morris, and moved there in the spring of 1983.

I was excited to be working at a new place. I was flying a bigger airplane that could do more work, and I was getting paid more money. I thought I had the world by the tail, but I was wrong; on the second day of July, I crashed the airplane.

It was a miserably hot day. I had two small fields to spray; I loaded so I could spray both of them with one load. The airplane was feeling extremely heavy and I was having trouble just keeping it flying. I finished the first field, and was relieved to be flying with a lighter load. I thought that the worst was over, but it was only the beginning.

When I arrived at the second field, I circled it once to check for obstacles and the best way to spray it. There was a row of trees bordering the field that I would have to go over. As I made my approach, lined up for the first pass, the airplane started to drop out of the sky for no apparent reason. I was not quite beyond the trees and I settled into the upper branches. I could see the branches emerging over the top of the lower wing, as the airplane smashed through them. The impact was slowing me down even more. I hit the emergency-dump lever, jettisoning my load, but the airplane continued dropping right to the ground. I bounced a little, but the wheels kept dragging through the crop, causing the speed to slow even further. I knew that I was not going to be able to get the airplane flying again, so I reduced power.

This caused the airplane to slow at a much quicker rate, and the tail of the airplane started to rise. I held the control stick all the way back trying to get the tail to lower, but then it continued to rise until the airplane flipped upside-down.

The plane was a total wreck and I was out of a job; I did not get hurt physically, but emotionally I was a mess, and became very depressed.

To try to make some income, I worked out a lease arrangement with Benson on their airplane, but could only use it when they were not. It was a scheduling nightmare, and I abandoned the idea. I flew my boss' plane some, but I developed a cyst on the back of my left knee and couldn't do that anymore either. So, I took a job helping a construction crew build a new electric power line.

One day while on the job, I felt a twinge in my hip. I thought, *I must have stepped wrong or something.* By the end of the day I could hardly walk on it, and by the time I drove home I couldn't walk at all. I had to crawl up to the house to get Julie to take me to the hospital. I was diagnosed with a staph infection that had settled out in my right hip socket. The next day, a surgeon cut the side of my hip open, and left it that way for three days to drain out fluids that had accumulated. Then it was back into surgery to sew it up, with suction tubes left inside to further drain out the infection. I was in the hospital for ten days, treated as an outpatient for several weeks and was on crutches for a couple months more.

I was beginning to think God had it in for me, and I couldn't wait for the year to be over.

I was broke, I had huge hospital bills to pay and I was out of a job. I was in such a deep depression that most of the time I just sat and stared into space.

In the spring, I took a job back with Benson Flying Service.

Although I really didn't want to, I had to do something to make some money, and they offered to hire me back.

As we were moving from our house in Morris, I paused in the empty kitchen, in total despair, and prayed to God. I asked Him, *Is this just too much to ask for? All I wanted is a simple life, with a comfortable home, and a job that I enjoy. Did you have to take everything away from me?* As I was praying, I felt a jolt pass through my body, and instantly a total peace filled me completely. My depression left me, and I knew that God would make everything work out if I trusted him. Jesus says in The Gospel of John, "I am leaving you with a gift—peace of mind and heart. And the peace I give isn't like the peace the world gives. So don't be troubled or afraid" (John 14:27 NLT).

I knew that I had been touched by God, and I had no doubt that there was a God that cared about me, and that He would provide for me completely if I trusted Him, and He did.

We moved to Benson, and put our house up for sale. A local family moved in with the intention to buy the place, but they could not get financing. My boss in Morris got sick and could not fly anymore. So after a busy summer working at Benson, we moved back to Morris to our same house and job. The next year we bought the business in Morris, and ran it for thirteen years. God blessed us with many good years, and the business kept growing to the point where I had to hire another pilot. I had two spray planes for crop dusting, and a twin-engine airplane that I used on business flights for area companies. I was also very busy flight instructing.

We had three wonderful children born to us over the years and things couldn't be better. God blessed us in every way. But I became just like the Israelites: the more God blessed them, the less they needed God, and soon they turned from God, and found enjoyment in worldly things. I was going down the same path. The path that leads to death and destruction! And I was oblivious to it. I was drinking heavily, partying, and doing whatever brought me personal pleasure. I was living life only to please myself.

Then one morning, after a night out on the town, while on a flight to Colorado, I received a revelation from God. He gave to me a vision. This vision did not come from my head, like a dream does; this vision came from my heart. God showed me standing at the very edge of the pit of hell, and I knew that if I took one more step in the direction that I was going I would lose my eternal soul forever. Then God showed me the light inside of me that comes from Him. This light was just a flicker; it was nearly completely snuffed out. Paul writes, "The wages of sin is death" (Romans 6:23), and I was as close to spiritual death as I could get.

I knew that I needed to turn from my sin and return to God. I began to pray often, asking God for forgiveness for the sins that I had committed. Yet, I continued living a life of sin. It seemed like I could not break free from the chains that bound me. I was a slave to sin, and it was controlling my life (just like it talks about in the book of Romans, chapters six and eight).

In the meantime, God continued to bless me, even though I did not deserve it, because God does not go back on His promises. This is the grace of God talked about in Romans 11:6, "free and undeserved." But God does not let sin go unpunished, or He would not be a just God.

> I show this unfailing love to many thousands by forgiving every kind of sin and rebellion. Even so I do not leave sin unpunished, but I punish

> the children for the sins of their parents to the third and fourth generations.
>
> Exodus 34:7 (NLT)

In 1995, when everything seemed to be going well, God's punishment came.

That spring, I sold my twin-engine airplane to buy a turbine engine for my spray plane.

In mid-summer, I crashed the spray plane and totaled it out. It happened when I initiated the pull-up after the last pass on the field. The nose started to pitch-up, then suddenly pitched-down, along with the right wing. The wing and nose of the airplane struck the ground simultaneously, sending the airplane into a series of cartwheels. Then the airplane went inverted, sliding across the ground on its top; the windshield broke out and dirt began filling the cockpit, hitting me in the face. I thought I was going to die for sure (by being buried alive), but then it came to a stop. I was hanging upside down from the seatbelts and was feeling completely disoriented. I released the belts and crawled out of the side door. I was bruised and sore, but otherwise I was unharmed. The wreckage did not even resemble an airplane anymore. The only things that saved me were the roll-cage built into the cockpit, and the hand of God.

Two weeks later my hired pilot, Kyle, crashed his airplane, when he fell out of a turn while spraying a field.

I was left with a two-airplane business and no airplanes; so I leased an airplane to cover my work. About a week later, while flying the rental plane, the engine started to sputter, and then quit completely. Usually, I am very nervous when something like this happens, and my mind is racing to think of what I need to do next, but I was completely numb.

On the way to the ground, the only thing that went

through my mind was, *God I can't take anymore of this! If I wreck this airplane, I am walking away from this business, and I am never looking back.*

I first picked out a hayfield to land in, but could see that I was not going to make it that far. I then chose an oats field that was cut and lying in swaths. The farmer was combining the oats as I landed. The field was very short with trees on the far end. I touched down and rolled to a stop just before hitting the trees. I praised the LORD for helping me land safely and finished the season with that airplane; however, all day and night I was in extreme pain from my previous accident. I never gave my body time to heal, and I paid dearly for it. Besides being stiff and sore in about every muscle of my body, I had severe cramps in both legs that continued day and night. That was another year I was glad to see come to an end.

I eventually sold my business in Morris, to Kyle. Looking back now, I realize I lost almost everything I had because of my sinful life. But because God is merciful, and abounding in steadfast love, and never goes back on His promises, He blessed me even more.

I ended up moving to Staples, Minnesota, where I started a better business, with a bigger and better airplane. The first couple of years at Staples were very busy. I had hoped to do sixty thousand acres per year. I was doing about seventy-five thousand acres, and hiring Kyle to do another twenty thousand.

I was working too hard, and it was taking a toll on my relationship with my wife. I was still a slave to the sin in my life. I just could not break the chains that bound me.

Finally, one night I came to God in prayer and asked God if He could please take this all away from me. I was so tired of this sinful life. It was controlling every part of me, including my thoughts and dreams.

I thought that God would just remove these things from my life by some miracle, but like it says in the Book of Isaiah, "'For my thoughts are not your thoughts, neither are your ways my ways,' declares the LORD. As the heavens are higher than the earth, so are my ways higher than your ways and my thoughts than your thoughts" (Isaiah 55:8–9, NIV).

The next morning Julie woke up absolutely mad at me, and I had no idea why. I didn't know it at the time, but I believe that God put what I call a "veil of anger" over her. No matter what I said or did, Julie became more and more angry with me. In fact, the longer I was in her presence, the madder she became. A few days later she left home. She said that she just had to get away for a while. I didn't know where she went, nor when, or if she was coming back.

I was going crazy. I was in the middle of the spraying season, the kids had just started school, and my airplane was broken down with a fuel-control problem. It was probably a good thing that the airplane was broken, because I was in no shape to fly anyway. I hired Kyle to do the work for me. Besides, I had to take care of the kids.

After five days she returned home. I had such mixed feelings; I was so happy that she was back, but I was also upset with her for leaving and just dumping everything on me.

Our marriage started falling apart. The harder I tried to fix things, the worse they got. I started praying to God continuously. I also started reading a Bible we had in the house, to see if I could find any answers to why this was happening. It was like reading the directions of how to live my life, after I had messed everything up, and was stuck. Slowly, the answers were being revealed to me.

About this same time, my youngest son received a Bible

from our church. On the way home, I mentioned to him how blessed he was to have a Bible given to him. I told him I was almost thirty-nine years old, and still didn't have a Bible of my own. My wife overheard us talking, and went out and bought one for me. She presented it to me for my birthday. It was the best gift I have ever received.

Our marriage was continuing in a downward spiral, even with going to counseling. We were sleeping in separate beds now. Julie could hardly stand to be in the same room with me anymore.

Our counselor finally decided we should separate; he said it would be best if I were to leave. It was the last thing I wanted to do, but reluctantly I gave in.

I started looking for a place to move to. I could not find any place decent in the whole town. One day I stopped by my neighbor's house to see if they had a room to rent, because I knew they had boarded someone there before. I remember telling Ron as I stood on his doorstep, "I can see the love of Jesus in your eyes, and I want that too" (I said this because I could see the "light of Christ" in him).

He said, "You can," and he brought me in, and prayed with me, and offered me a room to stay in. Then he gave me a Bible study by Henry Blackaby and Claude King, called *Experiencing God*.

I didn't know it at the time, but Ron told me later that he had been doing this same Bible study when I knocked at the door. In the study, the authors said God is working everywhere, and that we need to look for where God is at work, and join him. Ron was in prayer asking God to show him where He was working, when I showed up at the door. God was clearly at work here!

By now, Julie wanted me out of the house immediately. So, I moved my clothes and a few things over to Ron's house.

I was so distraught, depressed, and heart-broken, that I could only sleep about two hours each night. I had to force myself to eat. I could barely function as a person. I prayed, and read my Bible, and I cried my heart out continuously to God. I was seeking His help with all of my heart, but because of my past sins God had turned away from me.

You see, we can't expect God to come to our rescue when we have been walking in disobedience to God. God says through Isaiah, "Listen! The LORD is not too weak to save you, and he is not becoming deaf. He can hear you when you call. But there is a problem—your sins have cut you off from God. Because of your sin, he has turned away and will not listen anymore" (Isaiah 59 1–2, NLT).

Sin comes between God and us. Then when we need Him to help straighten things out, after our sin gets us in trouble, He is not listening to us anymore. "For a brief moment I abandoned you, but with great compassion I will take you back. In a moment of anger I turned my face away for a little while. But with an everlasting love I will have compassion on you,' says the LORD your Redeemer" (Isaiah 54:7–8, NLT).

He allows us to suffer the pain and consequences of our sin. But, He does not stay angry with us forever, because He is a loving God, full of mercy and forgiveness. He will listen again, when the time is right.

> But if from there you seek the LORD your God, you will find him if you look for him with all your heart and with all your soul. When you are in distress and all these things have happened to you, then in later days you will return to the LORD your God and obey him. For the LORD

> your God is a merciful God; he will not abandon
> or destroy you…
>
> Deuteronomy 4:29–31 (NIV)

About a month after moving into his home, Ron asked me to go to a men's retreat sponsored by his church. I went with him, because I thought it would be a nice break, and I knew it would give me an opportunity to pray more for my marriage, with the help of many others.

The evening of the worship service I began to pray in earnest. I was sobbing and weeping as I prayed. I confessed to God all of my sins and I pleaded with Him, *I know what a mess I have made of my life.* I prayed, *Please help renew my marriage. I know that you can change the hearts of people in an instant if you want to. Please change my wife's heart, so that she will love me again.* I concluded with, *But, even if you don't, from now on I am going to follow you. Make me your servant LORD. Transform me into what you would have me to be.*

As soon as I finished this prayer, a very strange sensation came over me. I was burning up on the inside! I felt my skin to see if it was hot; it wasn't. I wasn't even sweating. This was coming from deep inside my body. I knew this was something supernatural! For about ten to twenty seconds, I felt like the burning bush that Moses saw. I felt like I was on fire, but was not consumed. I knew something had happened to me, but I didn't know what.

I went away from the retreat with a hunger for the Word of God. I not only read The Bible every chance I got, but I studied every word. And I had a new understanding of the Word. I could feel the Holy Spirit guiding and teaching me.

Before reading each day, I would ask the Holy Spirit to reveal God's truth to me. I was trying to find out what happened to me the night of the retreat. It took me eight months of studying before I realized what it was.

One night I was reading in the Book of Ezekiel. God said:

> Then I will sprinkle clean water on you and you will be clean. Your filth will be washed away, and you will no longer worship idols. And I will give you a new heart with new and right desires, and I will put a new spirit in you. I will take out your stony heart of sin and give you a new, obedient heart. And I will put my Spirit in you so you will obey my laws and do whatever I command.
>
> Ezekiel 36:25–27 (NLT)

When I read this, I instantly knew that this is what happened to me. God had forgiven me for my sins, and had given me a new heart, and a new spirit. He put His Spirit in me. I was like a new person. I also was given this assurance that I was now counted as one of God's children, or that I had been "saved."

Also, shortly after the retreat, I had this overwhelming desire to be baptized, even though I had already been baptized as a child. I didn't think a minister would baptize me again, so I baptized myself. I filled a bathtub with water, and got in. I poured water over my head and baptized myself "a disciple of Jesus Christ," in the name of the Father, the Son, and the Holy Spirit, and I asked God to cleanse me of my sin.

Afterwards, I realized this is because in the gospel of John, Jesus answered, "I tell you the truth, no one can enter the kingdom of God unless he is born of water and the Spirit (John 3:5, NIV).

In Jesus' time, baptism was used to symbolize the cleansing of sins, after repentance, and the joining of God's holy family.

I know that the sacrifice of Jesus on the cross, paid the penalty for my sins, but the guilt of my sins still remained until I was baptized. Afterwards, I felt like the stains of my sins had been washed from my soul and from this point on, my sins were forgotten by God, and I had been given a fresh start.

Like God says through Ezekiel, "Then I will sprinkle clean water on you and you will be clean. Your filth will be washed away" (Ezekiel 36:25, NLT).

And through Isaiah, "I-yes, I alone-am the one who blots out your sins for my own sake and will never think of them again" (Isaiah 43:25, NLT).

Peter writes, "And this is a picture of baptism, which now saves you by the power of Jesus Christ's resurrection. Baptism is not a removal of dirt from your body; it is an appeal to God for a clean conscience" (1Peter 3:21, NLT).

Even Paul wrote in Acts, "And now what are you waiting for? Get up, be baptized and wash your sins away, calling on his name" (Acts 22:16, NIV).

The scriptures also tell us in Romans:

> For we died and were buried with Christ by baptism. And Just as Christ was raised from the dead by the glorious power of the Father, now we also may live new lives. Since we have been united with him in his death, we will also be raised as he was. Our old sinful selves were crucified with Christ so that sin might lose its power in our lives. We are no longer slaves to sin. For when we died with Christ we were set free from the power of sin.
>
> Romans 6: 4–7 (NLT)

Baptism symbolizes putting our old sinful nature to death as we go under the water, and taking on a new life, lead by the Holy Spirit as we come up out of the water.

> Those who are dominated by the sinful nature think about sinful things, but those who are controlled by the Holy Spirit think about things that please the Spirit. If your sinful nature controls your mind, there is death...For the sinful nature is always hostile to God...That's why those who are still under the control of their sinful nature can never please God. But you are not controlled by your sinful nature. You are controlled by the Spirit if you have the Spirit of God living in you. (And remember that those who do not have the Spirit of Christ living in them do not belong to him at all.) And Christ lives within you, so even though your body will die because of sin, the Spirit gives you life because you have been made right with God...And just as God raised Christ Jesus from the dead, he will give life to your mortal bodies by this same Spirit living within you.
>
> Therefore, dear brothers and sisters, you have no obligation to do what your sinful nature urges you to do...But if through the power of the Spirit you put to death the deeds of your sinful nature, you will live. For all who are led by the Spirit of God are children of God.
>
> Romans 8:5–14 (NLT)

By the power of the Holy Spirit, because of Christ's sacrifice on the cross and through His baptism, I finally was freed from the power of sin. I had died to sin, so that I could live for Christ.

During this time, it also became my obsession to find out what salvation was all about and how to obtain it, so that everyone could know. But before I get into that, I would like to finish my story.

Several months passed by after the retreat, and my marriage was getting worse. My wife was pursuing divorce, and she did not want me to talk to her anymore.

I was a total wreck. I was fighting depression and anxiety, and I could not take any drugs to help me, because I would lose my medical certificate for flying if I did. I wasn't doing any flying at the time, but I turned down several offers to fly for other businesses temporarily, because I knew that I was in no shape to do so.

I knew I had to go on with my life; I needed to "Let Go and Let God." The more I tried to fix my marriage, the worse it was getting. I had been praying for God to fix my marriage, but I was not letting God fix it. I kept trying to do it myself.

Finally, I gave it all to God in prayer, and said, *I am not going to do anything anymore.* I told God, *I trust you to do what is best for me, and whatever happens to my marriage, will have to come from you. I will accept whatever you think is best for me. Let it happen according to your will.* And I left it in God's hands.

I had been looking into buying a house, because I could not find anything to rent. Shortly after this prayer, I had the feeling that God wanted me to buy the house I had been looking at, and to buy it now. I felt He wanted me to take a "leap of faith" and if I did this, everything would work out.

Many people told me this was a bad idea, but God's ways are not the same as mans' ways. I felt that God was testing me to see if I would follow Him, or follow men. I decided to follow God, and I bought the house.

I closed the deal on a Monday. I moved my things on Tuesday, and on Wednesday my wife called to ask me out to dinner for the night. I could hardly believe it because it had been several months since I had moved out and our relationship was deteriorating every day.

We went out, and that night seemed like a dream come true for me. It was as if we had never been separated at all, and we had so much fun. Julie stated that when I was moving my things, God just lifted this heavy burden of anger off of her and it was gone (God removed what I call the "veil of anger").

Our relationship returned to better than ever, seemingly overnight. The days ahead became better every day. Soon, I proposed to Julie and asked her to marry me all over again. I even presented her with a new engagement ring. She accepted, and on the day that we were scheduled to have our first divorce hearing, we renewed our wedding vows instead.

I know without a doubt that this could have only come from God! I give all the praise and glory to Him! It was because people were praying, and because God answers prayer, that our marriage was saved!

In the meantime, I continued studying The Bible every chance I got. I was reading it from cover to cover. I wanted to know all of the truth that the Word of God contained. I asked the Holy Spirit to guide me into truth, to teach me, and lead me through The Bible. I was just amazed at all the knowledge that was being revealed to me. I tried reading The Bible several times before, and I got very little out of it. But, this time was different; I completely understood everything that I read. I'm a slow reader, so it took me about a year to read the whole Bible.

About a week after I finished, a Spirit of God visited me in a dream (I refer to this spirit as "The Spirit of Truth"). He came to me carrying a basket full of scrolls (paper rolled-up with writings on them, that were tied with a ribbon).

I looked up at the spirit and asked, "What is this?"

He said, "These scrolls contain the spiritual truths of the universe. I want you to read them."

The first thought that came into my mind was, *Obviously this spirit doesn't know how slow of a reader I am*, because the first thing I blurted out was, "I will never be able to read all these before I wake up in the morning."

He said, "Yes you will."

I said, "Okay," and I began to read them one by one, setting them aside when I was done.

When I was about half done, I looked up at the spirit once more and said, "I will never be able to finish these before I wake up in the morning."

Again, he said, "Yes you will."

So, I continued reading. As I got done, I looked up at the spirit one last time and exclaimed, "You were right, I made it!"

Instantly my eyes opened and I sat up in bed, wide-awake. My first thought was, *Whoa- that really happened!*

I don't remember anything that I read that night, but I know that God did not put His Truth into my mind; He put it into my heart. And now His Words of Truth flow through me like blood through my veins.

I know that this really did happen to me, and God has gifted me with biblical knowledge and understanding. I also feel that He does not want me to keep this knowledge to myself, but to share it with others. I have since started teaching God's Word at every opportunity that presents itself. Even though I had never been in a Bible study with others, God empowered me with the ability to lead and teach Bible studies.

I don't tell you these things to boast about what God has done for me, but so that you will know that these things are available to all who seek them. Jesus says in the Book of Luke:

> So I say to you: Ask and it will be given to you; seek and you will find; knock and the door will be opened to you. For everyone who asks receives; those who seek find; and to those who knock, the door will be opened.

> "Which of you fathers, if your son asks for a fish, will give him a snake instead? Or if he asks for an egg, will give him a scorpion? If you then, though you are evil, know how to give good gifts to your children, how much more will your Father in heaven give the Holy Spirit to those who ask him!"
>
> Luke 11:9–13 (TNIV)

I asked God to show me the truth; and He gave me Truth (Jesus). So, ask the Holy Spirit to teach you the ways of God and to lead you into truth.

> But when he, the Spirit of Truth, comes, he will guide you into all truth. He will not speak on his own, he will speak only what he hears, and he will tell you what is yet to come. He will

> bring glory to me by taking from what is mine, and making it known to you. All that belongs to the Father is mine. That is why I said the Spirit will take from what is mine and make it known to you.
>
> John 16:13–15 (NLT)

> But God has revealed it to us by his Spirit. For who among men knows the thoughts of a man except the man's spirit within him? In the same way no one knows the thoughts of God except the Spirit of God. We have not received the spirit of the world but the Spirit who is from God, that we may understand what God has freely given us. This is what we speak, not in words taught us by human wisdom but in words taught by the Spirit, expressing spiritual truths in spiritual words. The man without the Spirit does not accept the things that come from the Spirit of God, for they are foolishness to him, and he cannot understand them, because they are spiritually discerned.
>
> 1 Corinthians 2:10–14 (NLT)

It's the Holy Spirit that teaches us the ways of God.

As I stated before, I had this obsession to find out how salvation is obtained. I wanted to know how one is "saved," and what it means to be a "born again" Christian.

I didn't understand how I could have missed the message of salvation for so long. After all I had been going to church my whole life. I always thought this "born again" stuff was for some "holier than thou" Christians who thought they were better than everyone else. I didn't know it was a real experience, until it happened to me.

I wasn't looking to be saved that night it happened to me. I didn't even understand what had happened. I just stumbled into it (or was lead into it by the Holy Spirit). I have been studying the Bible ever since this experience happened to me, and I have asked the Holy Spirit to show me the truth regarding these things. I hope to be able to teach you what I have learned, so that you may know how to obtain salvation for yourself.

First of all, salvation is a free gift from God. There is nothing you can do to earn your way into heaven. And this is not something we deserve. Paul states, "For it is by grace you have been saved, through faith—and this is not from yourselves, it is a gift of God—not by works so that no one can boast" (Ephesians 2:8–9, TNIV).

None of us is so righteous that we can save ourselves. None of us is worthy to stand in the presence of the Most Holy God. "All of us have become like one who is unclean, and all our righteous acts are like filthy rags; we all shrivel up like a leaf, and like the wind our sins sweep us away" (Isaiah 64:6, TNIV).

"For all have sinned; all fall short of God's glorious standard" (Romans 3:23, NLT).

So if none of us is worthy, then how can we be saved?

God saw that none of us could save ourselves, and so he sent his son, Jesus Christ, to save us.

"For God so loved the world that he gave his one and only Son, that whoever believes in him shall not perish but have eternal life. For God did not send his Son into the world to condemn the world, but to save the world through him" (John 3:16–17, TNIV).

"We are made right in God's sight when we trust in

Jesus Christ to take away our sins. And we all can be saved in this same way, no matter who we are or what we have done" (Romans 3:22, NLT).

"For God sent Jesus to take the punishment for our sins and to satisfy God's anger against us. We are made right with God when we believe that Jesus shed his blood, sacrificing his life for us" (Romans 3:25a, NLT).

"That if you confess with your mouth, 'Jesus is LORD,' and believe in your heart that God raised him from the dead, you will be saved. For it is with your heart that you believe and are justified, and it is with your mouth that you confess and are saved" (Romans 10:9–10, NIV).

Jesus is not one of the ways to be saved; He is the only way to salvation. It is by our faith in him that we are saved. Jesus answered, "I am the way and the truth and the life. No one comes to the Father except through me" (John 14:6, NIV).

Before the day of my salvation, I had accepted Christ as my Savior, but I was still lacking something; I was still being controlled by my sinful nature. It was because I had not yet surrendered to Jesus, as LORD, and I had not yet received the Holy Spirit.

The Holy Spirit showed me the sin in my life, and the need to repent. "Those whom I love I rebuke and discipline. So be earnest, and repent" (Revelation 3:19, NIV).

Listen to what the LORD says about repentance:

> "Therefore, O house of Israel, I will judge you, each one according to his ways, declares the Sovereign LORD. Repent! Turn away from all your offenses; then sin will not be your downfall. Rid yourselves of all the offenses you have committed, and get a new heart and a new spirit. Why will you die, O house of Israel? For I

> take no pleasure in the death of anyone, declares the Sovereign Lord. Repent and live!
>
> Ezekiel 18:30–32 (NIV)

Repentance means to turn around 180 degrees. No matter how far down the road we have gone that leads to death and destruction, we must turn from our sin, and come back to God. Then as he promised, "No matter how deep the stains of your sins, He can remove it. He can make you as clean as freshly fallen snow. Even if you are stained as red as crimson. He can make you as white as wool" (Isaiah 1:18, NLT).

> Draw close to God and God will draw close to you. Wash your hands, you sinners; purify your hearts, you hypocrites. Let there be tears for the wrong things you have done. Let there be sorrow and deep grief. Let there be sadness instead of laughter and gloom instead of joy. When you bow down before the Lord and admit your dependence on him, he will lift you up and give you honor.
>
> James 4:8–10 (NLT)

So we must confess our sins to God, put our faith in Jesus Christ, be baptized in His name, and God will take away all of our sins. They will be forgotten, and we will have a fresh start. This is what it means to be born again: getting a new heart, a new spirit, and a fresh start. We start completely new, just like when we were born. We are a new creation through Christ Jesus our Lord.

"But to all who believed him and accepted him, he gave the right to become children of God. They are reborn! This is not a physical birth resulting from human passion or plan—this rebirth comes from God" (John 1:12–13, NLT).

"For you have been born again. Your new life did not come from your earthly parents because the life they gave you will end in death. But this new life will last forever because it comes from the eternal, living Word of God" (1 Peter 1:23, NLT).

"I assure you, unless you are born again, you can never see the Kingdom of God" (John 3:3, NLT).

"The truth is, no one can enter the Kingdom of God without being born of water and the Spirit. Humans can reproduce only human life, but the Holy Spirit gives new life from heaven. So don't be surprised at my statement that you must be born again" (John 3:5–7, NLT).

We must be born again, and we must receive the Holy Spirit, which God will give us, if we ask Him, once we have put our trust in Him. And out of obedience to what God has called all Christians to do; we should be baptized in the name of the Father, the Son, and the Holy Spirit (Matthew 28:19).

Another thing we need to do to be saved is to commit our life to God, give control of our life to God, and submit to His will.

If Jesus laid down his life for us, can we offer anything less, but to devote our life back to Him?

> Then Jesus said to his disciples, "If anyone would come after me, he must deny himself and take up his cross and follow me. For whoever wants to save his life will lose it, but whoever loses his life for Me will find it. What good would it do for you to gain the whole world, but to lose your own soul in the process? Is anything worth more than your soul?"
>
> Matthew 16:24–26 (NLT)

Or in other words, we must live a God-centered life, rather than a self-centered life. We must first serve God, because as Jesus says, "No one can serve two masters. Either he will hate the one and love the other, or he will be devoted to the one and despise the other. You cannot serve both God and money (Matthew 6:24, NIV).

> "Do not store up for yourselves treasures on earth, where moth and rust destroy, and where thieves break in and steal. But store up for yourselves treasures in heaven, where moth and rust do not destroy, and where thieves do not break in and steal. For where your treasure is, there your heart will be also.
>
> Matthew 6:19–21 (NIV)

We do not need to worry about the things of this world that we need. God will provide all of them to us if we live for Him and make the Kingdom of God our primary concern (Matthew 6:32–33).

So, we must prioritize our lives daily, and think about the things that we devote our time and energy to, and make God the most important thing in our lives.

And please don't do like I did, and wait until God brings you to your knees completely broken, before you seek Him.

Finally, I want to leave you with the words that the Holy Spirit gave to me one night. These words were the answer to the things that I had been searching for about salvation. It was about 3:00 a.m. when these words came into my heart, and I had to get up right away and write them down.

*It's by the grace of God,
through the power of the Holy Spirit,
because of your faith in Jesus Christ,
you have been saved.*

A few years after being born-again, over a period of two years, God gave me a new song. The words just kept coming, until I had so many in my head that I decided to write them down. Once I started writing, it only took me about ten minutes to get it on paper.

God gave songs to many of the people in The Bible after doing a great work. A few examples of these are when God brought Israel thru the Red Sea, (Exodus 15). He gave Moses a new song before bringing Israel into the "Promised Land" (Deuteronomy 32). And in Judges 5 we see the "Song of Deborah" sung after leading Israel to victory over their enemies.

In Revelation 5, John tells us that we will all sing a new song to the Lamb when we get to heaven.

"Sing a new song to the LORD, for he has done wonderful deeds. His right hand has won a mighty victory; his holy arm has shown his saving power" (Psalm 98:1, NLT)!

Because God's Son Has Set You Free

By my sins, I was enslaved.
But by God's grace, I have been saved.
I was blind, but now I see,
Once was bound, but now set free.

Free to worship Him in truth.
Freed from my sins of youth.
Free to be all I can be,
Because God's Son has set me free.

It's by faith in what God's done,
When God sent His only son.
On the cross, He paid the price,
When for me, He gave his life.

Now through Him, I'm born again.
Now He even calls me friend.
And there's no greater sacrifice,
Than for a friend, to give your life.

So, I devote my life to Him.
I didn't decide this on a whim.
I weighed the cost, sought the reward.
And now Christ is my Light and Sword.

The Holy Spirit lives within.
He convicts me of my sin.
He shows me truth in God's way,
So from His path, I will not stray.

And now I wait for His return,
When all the world will finally learn
That Jesus Christ is the King,
And the Lord of everything.

And so I pray that you will too,
Accept the gift God gives to you.
Ask Jesus, into your heart,
And a new life, you too will start.

By your sins, you were enslaved.
But by God's grace, you have been saved.
You were blind but now you see,
Once were bound, but now set free.

Free to worship Him in truth.
Freed from your sins of youth.
Free to be all you can be.
Because God's Son has set you free.

By Faith

In the summer of 2002, I was out spraying potatoes with my Turbo Thrush airplane; it was 8:00 a.m. and the wind was already starting to blow.

Every morning throughout the summer, the first thing I do when I wake up at 4:30 a.m. is call the Flight Service Station and check on the weather. This morning, the forecast was for the wind to be blowing 15–25 mph by 9:00 a.m. I wasn't sure if I should even try to get any work done, but I finally decided to see if I could get a few loads sprayed out before the wind came up.

The spraying I had to do that day was from a satellite airport at Clarissa, MN, about twenty miles south of my home airport of Staples, Minnesota. After my first take-off, while I was climbing out, I could feel the wind pushing on the side of the airplane, as I had to crab into the wind (flying sideways), a considerable amount to hold my course. It was also quite turbulent. I thought to myself, *Flight Service is going to be right today!*

By 8:00 a.m. I could hardly hold onto the airplane as I pulled up over the trees bordering the potato field (because of the gusty winds aloft). I felt like a leaf being tossed about by the wind. Yet at the surface it was still workable for the moment. You can always feel the wind at altitude first, and then it slowly works its way down to the surface.

As I was spraying what I thought was going to be my last load for the day, my mind began to wander to the Bible study that I had been doing on the subject of faith. As part of this study I was reading about the miracles of Jesus.

I thought about the Roman officer in Matthew 8:5–13, who came to Jesus pleading for help for his sick servant back home. Jesus said that he would go to his house to heal him. But the centurion replied that he was not worthy for Jesus to come into his house, but if Jesus would just say the words from there his servant would be healed. Jesus exclaimed that he had not seen faith like this in all of Israel, and because of the Roman officer's faith, it would be done for him. And at that very hour his servant was healed.

Then I thought about the two blind men in Matthew 9:27–30 who asked Jesus to restore their sight. Jesus asked them if they believed that he could do this for them.

They replied, "Yes, Lord."

Jesus touched their eyes and said, "According to your faith, this will be done for you."

And they could see.

Then I thought of the woman in Mark 5:24–34 who had been bleeding for twelve years. She had spent all of her money on doctors, but nothing helped; in fact she was even worse.

She came to Jesus and thought, *If I could just touch His clothes I will be healed.* She worked her way through the crowd, touched Jesus' robe and instantly was healed.

Jesus felt power leave him and he turned to see who had touched him. After finding the woman, Jesus said to her,

"Daughter, your faith has healed you. Go in peace and be freed from your suffering."

I thought how each of these people believed something different, yet all were healed according to their faith. It was not about a certain method; *faith* was the key ingredient.

Then I thought of Jesus walking on the water in Matthew 14, and how Peter could walk on the water too, as long as he believed. But when he looked around and was distracted by the wind and the crashing waves, he began to doubt and also began to sink. Jesus helped him back into the boat and the wind died down.

I thought, *We are like that too. When the waves of life come crashing in around us, we begin to doubt, and we begin to sink.* I thought, *We too must keep our eyes focused on Jesus.*

Then, I remembered the story in Luke 8:22–25 of how Jesus rebuked the wind and it obeyed Him.

He and His disciples were crossing the lake when they were caught in a fierce storm. Jesus was asleep. His disciples were terrified and woke Him because they thought they were going to drown.

Jesus rebuked the wind and the waves, and suddenly the storm stopped and all was calm.

Then it was like a light bulb came on in my head; I thought, *Wow, God could do this for me too!*

Without hesitation, I prayed, "Dear heavenly Father, I know that you created the heavens and the earth and everything in them. I know that you are in control of everything, even the wind. If it be your will, would you please keep the wind down long enough for me to complete this work that you have called me to do."

Now, I confess that I was hoping that God would just keep the wind tolerable, but God did something even better.

When I said this prayer, the wind went completely calm and the air became as smooth as glass.

I got goose bumps all over my body and the hairs on the back of my neck were standing straight out. There was no frontal passage, no change in the wind direction and no reason for this to be happening, except that this was the work of God's hand, and I knew it. I couldn't help breaking into songs of praise and worship. I sang the words from "Shout to the Lord" by Darlene Zschech:

> *Shout to the Lord, all the earth, let us sing*
> *Power and Majesty, praise to the King;*
> *Mountains bow down and the seas will roar*
> *At the sound of Your name.*
> *I sing for joy at the work of your hands,*
> *Forever I'll love You, forever I'll stand*
> *Nothing compares to the promise I have in You.*

I have a smoker in my airplane, and I put out some smoke, to see if I was just imagining this. The smoke did not move. I've only seen it this calm a few times in twenty-seven years of spraying crops, and this went on for two hours.

As I sprayed out my last load, I praised God for revealing himself to me in such an awesome way, and as I finished the last pass of the day, I ended with, "Thank you, God, you can let her blow."

As I climbed to get altitude for the ride home, my wings began to rock. I looked down and the trees on the line-fence below me were waving like crazy! The bean field that I was flying over was rolling like a roaring sea! I was just in awe!

God released the wind he had been holding back and it hit me like water from a broken dam!

When I got back home, my wife asked, "How could you keep spraying in all this wind?"

I smiled and said, "It wasn't windy where I was." Then I told her what happened.

This experience really showed me the power of prayer, when combined with faith.

> "Have faith in God," Jesus answered. "I tell you the truth, if anyone says to this mountain, 'Go, throw yourself into the sea,' and does not doubt in his heart but believes that what he says will happen, it will be done for him. Therefore I tell you, whatever you ask for in prayer, believe that you have received it, and it will be yours."
>
> Mark 11:22–24 (NIV)

A few years later I had a similar experience as I was performing the first spray job of the year.

I had two fields to spray that were newly planted to trees the summer before. The grower had contracted me to apply herbicide on them to control weeds. The chemical that I was applying works in the soil and kills the weeds as they germinate; so it needs rain afterwards to soak it into the ground, but it can't be raining while I'm applying it because I won't be able to see through the windshield well enough to fly so close to the ground and maneuver around obstacles.

I completed the first field with no problems.

I started the second field, with two more loads left to go when rain clouds started closing in all around me.

I thought about when God held back the wind for me, and I prayed a similar prayer, because I thought, *God is in control of the rain, as well as the wind. This prayer worked once! Why not try it again?*

I prayed, "Dear Heavenly Father, I know that you created the heavens and the earth, and everything in them. I know that you are in control of everything. I know that you can control the rain, just as you did with the wind. If it be your will, please, don't let it rain on this field, until I finish this work that you have called me to do."

I had no doubt that God could hold back the rain if it was His will to do so; but would He?

Rain was closing in from the west and north sides of the field. I could see the heavy rain marching steadily across the land, swallowing up fields one by one as they disappeared from sight.

I kept on spraying and praying, trusting that God was going to answer my prayers.

Lightning struck the ground less than half a mile away to the northwest of where I was flying. I kept going. The heavy rain came right to the edge of the field and then miraculously, it stopped, as "the hand of God" held it from advancing any farther.

It reminded me of what God said to Job: "Who defined the boundaries of the sea as it burst from the womb, and as I clothed it with clouds and thick darkness? For I locked it behind barred gates, limiting its shores. I said, '*Thus far and no farther will you come.* Here your proud waves must stop!'" (Job 38:8–11, NLT).

"Who created a channel for the torrents of rain? Who laid out the path for the lightning?" (Job 38:25, NLT).

"Does the rain have a father? Where does dew come from?" (Job 38:28, NLT).

"Can you shout to the clouds and make it rain? Can

you make lightning appear and cause it to strike as you direct?"(Job 38:34–35, NLT)

I knew that God was orchestrating everything just like these verses say; He was holding back the rain just as He holds back the boundaries of the sea and He was channeling the torrents of rain and directing the lightning strikes. He is in control of everything!

I finished the first load on the field, but I still had two more loads to go in order to complete the job. I headed back to the airport, flying through the driving rain. I circumnavigated the heavy showers, trying to find a channel of lighter rain that I could see to fly through. God showed me the way. It was raining so hard that I had my windshield wiper on full speed, and I put my igniters on so that my engine would not flameout (that's when the engine is taking in so much water that it drowns out the fire and the engine quits; the igniters keep the fire lit).

When I got back to the airport, Craig, the guy I hired to load me, asked, "Do you want to keep going?"

I said, "Yeah, load her up."

He asked, "How can you continue spraying with all of this rain around?"

I smiled and said, "It's not raining where I'm spraying."

Then I dialed up the color radar on my cell-phone to see what it looked like. I was surprised to see that there was rain everywhere in the area except for a small dot, which I believed to be the field I was spraying.

Now, when I decide to take off with a full load, I am committed to getting that load sprayed out, because it is very difficult to land again with a full load. I will only do this in an emergency. In fact, during an emergency the previous year (when a side-panel tore loose form the airplane while in-flight), I tried landing with a full load, and went off the side of the runway and ended up in a bean field. So it was by faith that I loaded the airplane with another load, and it was by faith that I took off now, believing that God was going to continue to hold back the rain.

It was raining moderately the entire way back to the field. When I arrived, lightning was now striking on both ends of the field and it was raining on all four sides, but it was not raining on the field! There was just enough room on the ends of the field for me to do my turnarounds.

I was just amazed and in awe of the power of God being displayed right before my eyes. It was so incredible that I could hardly believe what I was seeing. I imagined that this must have been what it was like for the Israelites, when God divided the Red Sea and they crossed through on dry ground with walls of water on each side.

And yet, at the same time, I had no doubt in me and was not surprised that God could do just what He says He can do in The Scriptures.

I was just praising God over and over, thanking Him for answering my prayer with this awesome display of His power.

And again, I had to go back to the airport for one more load. God continued holding back the rain.

After completing the job, I made my way back home through the rain the entire forty-five miles. I shut down the engine, put the airplane in the hangar and dialed up the radar screen one more time. The entire screen was now completely filled in with heavy rain. I thanked the LORD for all that He had done.

Again, this showed me the importance of faith. The scriptures tell us, "Without faith it is impossible to please God, because anyone who comes to him must believe that he exists and that he rewards those who earnestly seek him" (Hebrews 11:6, NIV).

So, what is faith?

"Faith is being sure of what we hope for and certain of what we do not see" (Hebrews 11:1, NIV).

It is trusting in God with our whole heart and soul.

In the book of Joshua, chapter three, when the Israelites came to the Jordan River to enter the "Promised Land," God told Joshua to have the Levites carry the "Ark of the Covenant" into the river, and then God would hold back the waters until all the Israelites had safely crossed.

Now, it was harvest time and the banks of the river were overflowing, so the current had to be very strong. Yet, God did not say he would hold the water back first and then they could cross on dry ground. No, they had to take the first step; they had to jump into the raging river with both feet, and then God would hold back the water.

This is the kind of faith that pleases God, when we hold nothing back and jump in with both feet!

Jesus says, "I tell you the truth, anyone who will not receive the kingdom of God like a little child will never enter it" (Mark 10:15, NIV).

We must have faith like a child: not questioning or doubting—just believing and trusting.

Another thing that I noticed while studying The Bible is that God tests our faith at times to see if we really do believe. Like when Joshua came to the city of Jericho after crossing the Jordan River. There were fortified walls built around the entire city. God told Joshua to march around the city one time for six days blowing a ram's horn. On the seventh day to march around it seven times, blowing the ram's horn, and on the seventh time to give a mighty shout, and the walls of the city would fall down. And that is what happened!

But, I am sure that Joshua had lots of men in his army

asking, "What are we doing?" They must have thought that Joshua had lost his mind.

Can you imagine the United States Army humbling themselves enough to do something like this?

God tests our faith, sometimes by asking us to do things that by human standards seem ridiculous or even foolish!

I know now that God was testing my faith when He told me to buy the house while I was separated from my wife. He placed it on my heart that if I bought this house that the problems that were separating us would be resolved. It made no sense, and everyone that I asked for advice about this told me that I shouldn't do it, but I chose to follow God rather than men (even though it seemed foolish at the time), and I bought the house. And everything worked out just as God told me it would.

I had a young girl named Hannah in my youth group until she graduated and went off to college. I've known her since she was in seventh grade. She even worked for me a couple of summers. She has great faith, but it too was tested in her senior year of high school. Here is her story, written in her own words:

> I find that God often places obstacles in front of us and challenges us in the things we are most passionate about. Running is one of my greatest passions. During my senior year cross-country season, I had the opportunity to have God challenge me and then perform a miracle through me.
>
> There is no doubt in my mind that God had a profound purpose when he pointed our cross-country team to Matthew 19:26 for the 2005

season verse; it states, *"With man it is impossible, but with God all things are possible."* And this is why I am convinced.

It all started about a month into the season, just when we were beginning competitive meets. For some reason my legs were not as graceful, loose, or light. My legs were not moving as fast as they had in the past—even weeks before. I pushed as hard as I could, but nothing helped. I could start a race or practice near the front of the pack, but a little ways into it, I'd fall back. It felt like ropes with bricks were tugging at me from behind. I just assumed I wasn't having a good season and hopefully I'd get out of this slump.

Well, that never really happened. About two weeks before the state meet, we were doing a speed workout (1000 meter repeats). Once again I could maintain a fast pace for the first lap, but then I would get slower and slower, and by the end of the thousand meters I would practically be jogging. My coach decided something had to be wrong, so he put me in his car and we rushed to the clinic. After testing my blood, the results showed that my iron was extremely low, thus I had iron-deficiency anemia.

It was nice to know something was wrong, so I could try to fix it. The only problem was that I only had two weeks until state and everything the doctors were trying didn't work. All I could do was take iron tablets and hope for a little improvement.

Throughout this whole time I was really frustrated. It was hard to understand why I had to run this badly my last season of high school. Every race and practice I feared. I would get up to the starting line and pray, *Lord, please give me the strength and courage to finish.*

The only thing getting me through was encouragement from people, and my relationship with the Lord. Many people comforted me and prayed for me.

About half way through the season, I received this e-mail from Ken Peterson:

September 30, 2005

Hi, Hannah:
I'm writing to you to give you some encouragement. The last few weeks that I have seen you, I sense that you are struggling with life. Though you smile on the outside, I can see that something is troubling you deep inside. I know that things are not going well with you in cross-country, and I don't know if this has something to do with it, or if it is something more.

Are you feeling that God is not listening to your prayers?

He is always listening, but sometimes He doesn't answer them the way that we would like. God says, "My thoughts are completely different from yours, and my ways are far beyond anything you could imagine. For just as the heavens are higher than the earth, so are my ways higher than your ways and my thoughts higher than your thoughts" (Isaiah 55:8–9).

I feel in my heart that God has great plans for you, Hannah. I don't know what they are, but I know that God tests us at times to see where our hearts are at.

"The eyes of the LORD search the whole earth in order to strengthen those whose hearts are fully committed to him" (2 Chronicles 16:9).

I know that if you trust Him fully that He will not let you down. I believe that if you stay committed to Him even in tough times, that God will always be there for you. Who knows, He may be setting you up to do a great miracle through you in which you have this miraculous recovery and start winning races, and you will be a great witness to Him.

These things could be happening to you for a multitude of reasons, but I know that if you continue trusting Him and seeking the answers, God will reveal them to you in His timing.

Then it was the night before state and I decided to spend some quality time with God. I began to write a prayer in my notebook and this is the last thing it read:

> *I have just one request. LORD, if you could do anything, I'd have you help me run an amazing race tomorrow. The reason I would love this is that it would be a miracle. People could come to know you. I could tell people the only way I did it was God. LORD, think of how great it would be. I pray that I'll keep up with our four other girls (on our team) or be in the top 25, something that would show how great you are. Help me believe. I trust in you and pray that my eyes will stay focused on you from start to finish. Help me not to get discouraged, but stay positive and know that you are God. Thank you that you are going to create a testimony through me. Thank you, Jesus.*

The next morning it was time to race. I was scared to death. I didn't even run at sections and my times this season would have put me in about 85th place. My heart pounded and I cried out to God.

As the gun went off my legs gracefully flowed, feeling as light as feathers. I ran past the half mile and still wasn't hitting a wall. This was unusual; normally my legs were dead and heavy by the quarter mile mark. Throughout the whole race my legs were light and quick. The only things slowing me down this time were my heart and lungs! Anyway, I finished the race strong and my time was fast enough for medalist honors. I placed eighth, which is the last place to go up on the awards stand.

People stared in awe and confusion. When they asked how I did it, my only response was, "It was a God thing!"

Lesson Learned: Often times we try to do things on our own and nothing gets accomplished. We come to God as a last resort, when none of the other options are working. In reality, God should be the first person we turn to. He is all-powerful and His miracles didn't end in Bible stories. He is still alive, and performing miracles today. If we have faith the size of a mustard seed, He can do the impossible.

"With man it is impossible, but with God all things are possible"

(Matthew 19:26).

So, what good is faith? Is it so we may receive a miracle from God?

Maybe, but what's more important is that it's faith that justifies us before God, and then we are open to experiencing God in an intimate and personal way.

The greatest reward of faith is our salvation that comes through faith.

> That if you confess with your mouth, "Jesus is LORD," and believe in your heart that God raised him from the dead, you will be saved. For it is with your heart that you believe and are justified, and it is with your mouth that you confess and are saved. As the Scripture says, Anyone who trusts in him will never be put to shame.
>
> Romans 10:9–11(NIV)

It's our faith in what Jesus did (when He died and rose again), that justifies us before God, or in other words, it's what makes us right with God. And it's by proclaiming this with our mouth that we show that we really do believe!

> By faith Abraham, when called to go to a place he would later receive as his inheritance, obeyed and went, even though he did not know where he was going. By faith he made his home in the Promised Land like a stranger in a foreign country... By faith Abraham, even though he was past age—and Sarah herself was barren—was enabled to become a father because he considered him faithful who had made the promise. And so from this one man... came descendants as numerous as the stars in the sky and as countless as the sand on the seashore.
>
> Hebrews 11:8–12 (NIV)

It was because of Abraham's faith in God, that he obeyed and left his country to follow God to a new place. And because of Abraham's faith, God made him the father of a new nation and gave him children, even though he and his wife were beyond the age of being able to have children.

> What then shall we say that Abraham, our forefather, discovered in this matter? If, in fact, Abraham was justified by works, he had something to boast about—but not before God. What does the Scripture say? "Abraham believed God, and it was credited to him as righteousness."
>
> Now when a man works, his wages are not credited to him as a gift, but as an obligation. However, to the man who does not work but trusts God who justifies the wicked, his faith is credited as righteousness.
>
> Romans 4:1–5 (NIV)

It's not by our good works that we are made right with God, and it is not by being a good person. It's by faith in what Christ did for us, not by what we do for God, that makes us acceptable to Him.

> It was not through law that Abraham and his offspring received the promise that he would be heir of the world, but through the righteousness that comes by faith. For if those who live by law are heirs, faith has no value, and the promise is worthless, because law brings wrath. And where there is no law there is no transgression.

> Therefore, the promise comes by faith, so that it may be by grace and may be guaranteed to all Abraham's offspring—not only to those who are of the law but also to those who are of the faith of Abraham.
>
> Romans 4:13–16(NIV)

During Abraham's time, God's law (including the Ten Commandments), had not even been given yet (this happened later, in Moses' time). So, we know that it's by faith, and not by obeying the law, that we are made right with God. Salvation comes to us as a gift, by grace, because of faith. In other words, salvation is not something that we deserve and it is not something that we can earn. It is by faith in what God did, when He sent His only Son into the world to pay the penalty for our sins (by dying on the cross), that we are made right with God.

> Before this faith came; we were held prisoners by the law, locked up until faith should be revealed. So the law was put in charge to lead us to Christ that we might be justified by faith. Now that faith has come, we are no longer under the supervision of the law. You are all sons of God through faith in Christ Jesus.
>
> Galatians 3:23–26(NIV)

Now we know that whatever the law says, it says to those who are under the law, so that every mouth may be silenced and the whole world held accountable to God. Therefore no one will be declared righteous in his sight by observing the law; rather, through the law we become conscious of sin.

Romans 3:19–20 (NIV)

The law was given to convict us of our sin and to make us realize our need for a Savior!

> "Until faith in Christ was shown to us as the way of becoming right with God, we were guarded by the law. We were kept in protective custody, so to speak, until we could put our faith in the coming Savior."

Galatians 3:23 (NLT)

But now God has shown us a way to be made right with him without keeping the requirements of the law, as was promised in the writings of Moses and the prophets long ago. We are made right with God by placing our faith in Jesus Christ. And this is true for everyone who believes, no matter who we are.

For everyone has sinned; we all fall short of God's glorious standard. Yet God, with undeserved kindness, declares that we are righteous. He did this through Christ Jesus when he freed us from the penalty for our sins. For God presented Jesus as the sacrifice for sin. People are made right with God when they believe that Jesus sacrificed his life, shedding his blood. This

> sacrifice shows that God was being fair when he held back and did not punish those who sinned in times past, for he was looking ahead and including them in what he would do in this present time. God did this to demonstrate his righteousness, for he himself is fair and just, and he declares sinners to be right in his sight when they believe in Jesus.
>
> Can we boast, then, that we have done anything to be accepted by God? No, because our acquittal is not based on obeying the law. It is based on faith. So we are made right with God through faith and not by obeying the law.
>
> Romans 3:21–28 (NLT)

We are made right with God through faith in what Christ did for us, not by our own good deeds.

"For it is by grace you have been saved, through faith—and this not from yourselves, it is the gift of God—not by works, so that no one can boast" (Ephesians 2:8–9, NIV).

The Scriptures also tell us that if anyone cares to boast, he should boast only in what God has done, not in what we have done (1 Corinthians 1:31), for no one has the power to save himself.

Therefore, I pray that you will accept the free gift that God has given to you, and that through faith, you will believe that God has given His son for you as atonement for your sins. That you will believe that Jesus is the Son of God and that He shed His blood, by dying on the cross for you, and that he rose from the dead three days later, and that He ascended into heaven and sits at the right hand of the Father. I pray that you will invite Him into your heart, and make him your Savior, and LORD of your life. If you believe these things, proclaim them to God in prayer today! Then tell others of this "good news," of salvation that comes through Jesus Christ! Amen.

"But when I, the Son of Man, return, how many will I find who have faith?" (Luke 18:8b, NLT).

Obedience

In the last chapter I wrote about how we are saved by faith. Yet if you read in the book of James 2:14–26, it tells us that faith without "good deeds" is dead. In this chapter I am going to explore how this is, and what role "good deeds" play in the life of a Christian.

One of the things I've always struggled with throughout my life and faith journey is that I was taught as a child we are saved by doing good works. I thought that I had to earn my salvation by going to church every Sunday and living a good life by keeping the Ten Commandments and being a good person. I thought that if I did these things, then I would go to heaven. The problem with this is I knew that I could never be good enough; I could never live up to God's holy standards.

Then I began to think, "God is never going to save me, so what difference does it matter what I do?" So, I turned to a life of sin.

Then later, when I turned back to God, I found it was by God's grace (which means that it is free and undeserved), and it is by the work of the Holy Spirit in us, and it is by our faith in what Jesus Christ did on the cross, that we are saved.

Paul says in Ephesians 2:8–9 (paraphrased by me), that it is by the grace of God, through faith, we have been saved, not by our good works, so that no one can boast about what they have done to gain their salvation. Salvation is a gift from God, not something that we earn.

Yet, James says that faith without good deeds is dead. This seemed like a contradiction to me. Some churches teach that we are saved by good deeds, and others teach that we are saved by faith alone. I began to pray about this, and I asked God to show me the truth regarding these things. You will have to stick with me for a couple more chapters to find out the whole truth in what God showed me as I studied His Word. For now, we are going to look at works.

James is right when he says in chapter 2, verse 19, that faith alone is not enough, that even the demons believe in God. They even refer to Jesus as "The Son of God," such as in Matthew 8:29, and in Mark 3:11, yet they will not be saved.

The Old Testament is filled with messages from God, through the prophets, telling men to turn from their wicked ways.

God speaks very clearly to us in Ezekiel 18, of how He is going to judge each of us by our deeds. He tells us that an evil person that turns from his sin and turns to God will live, but that if a righteous person turns to evil, that he will surely die. God tells us to repent and live.

When John the Baptist started his ministry, his message was that men must repent, or turn from their sins and turn to God.

Then Jesus said to his disciples, "If anyone would come after me, he must deny himself and take up his cross and follow me.

For whoever wants to save his life will lose it, but whoever loses his life for me will find it" (Matthew 16:24–25, NIV).

Henry Blackaby wrote in the book *Experiencing God*, "The very essence of sin is a shift from God-centeredness to self-centeredness."

Through this, I realized that sin is basically turning away from God and following our own evil desires. As James tells us, "Temptation comes from the lure of our own evil desires" (James 1:14, NLT).

Following our own selfish desires is saying that we know better than God. It is really the same thing that Satan did (putting himself above God); and this is why God threw him out of heaven.

Repentance is turning away from following self, and turning back to God (following God's ways).

And we know that sin leads to death. The Scriptures say, "For the wages of sin is death; but the gift of God is eternal life through Jesus Christ our LORD" (Romans 6:23, KJV).

Repentance leads to life. That is what Jesus meant when he said in Matthew 16:24–25, we must deny self (repent), pick up our cross (it is not going to be easy), and follow Him (turn to God), or we would lose our eternal soul.

If we try to live our life by following our own evil desires, it will lead to the death of our souls, but if we repent (give up our own selfish desires and live our life for Jesus), it will lead to eternal life.

It looks something like this: *Sin* is turning away from *God* and following *self*, which leads to *death*. *Repentance* is turning away from *self* and back to *God*, which leads to *life*.

In the parable of the Sheep and the Goats in Matthew 25:31–46, Jesus teaches us that those who do good deeds will go into heaven and those who do not will go into eternal punishment.

Now going back to James' teachings in 2:21–22, he is telling us that Abraham was declared right with God by what he *did*, and that Abraham trusted God so much that he was willing to do whatever God asked him to do. He gives us another example of this in James 2:25 when Rahab was made right before God by what she *did*.

Going by these examples, I continued to study the works of other great patriarchs of the Bible in Hebrews 11, and I started to see a pattern emerging. Like it says in Hebrews 11:7, that it was by faith that Noah built an ark to save his family from the flood, He *obeyed* God... and in Hebrews 11:8 it says, it was by faith that Abraham *obeyed* when God called him to leave home.

So we see both faith and obedience in all these examples. These patriarchs believed what God told them and then they did it.

Now, suppose that Noah believed that God wanted him to build an ark, but then did not *obey* God, and did not build the ark. Do you think that God would have saved Noah and his family? Or, would they have perished in the flood with the rest? I believe they would have perished.

And if Abraham believed that God wanted him to leave his country and go to a new land, but Abraham had not obeyed and had not left his home would God have still made him the father of a great nation? I don't think so.

I remember watching Indiana Jones as he searched for the "Holy Grail" in the movie *Indiana Jones and the Last Crusade*. He was required to take a "leap of faith" by stepping off the edge of a cliff to pass across a great chasm to the cliff on the other side. Indy did not know that there was a seemingly invisible bridge crossing the gap. He had to take that first step to find this out. Now, it's one thing for Indy to say that he believed, but it took a lot more courage to actually take that first step.

God wants us to step out in faith in this same way. It's one thing to say that we believe, it is another to actually live out our faith.

It was one thing for Abraham to believe that God wanted him to sacrifice his son Isaac, but it took courage to take that leap of faith and actually take Isaac up the mountain, lay him on the altar and draw out his knife to kill him. We know that God stopped him at this point and did not let Abraham complete this test, because God knew that Abraham was indeed, faithful and obedient.

I believe that God will test each of us in some way and at some time, to find out if we have this same kind of faith and obedience.

Like when God asked me to take a leap of faith and buy the house, while my wife and I were separated, I believed God and I obeyed God when I actually went out and bought the house.

So you see, these examples of "obedience to what God has called us to do" are a demonstration of our faith. In other words, it is the acting out of what we believe.

Now is there a difference between good works and obedience? Yes, I believe there is. The difference lies in the motive of our heart.

If God calls us to do a particular thing, either directly, or by burdening our heart with some assignment or through His Word, then it is through obedience that we go and accomplish what God has asked us to do.

Good works, on the other hand, are things that we "dream up" that we can do for God. And they may be very good things and it seems that by doing these things we will be pleasing God. But this may not be what God has asked us to do.

In other words, works are things that we decide will be pleasing to God—then we pray and ask God to bless them. This is us leading and asking God to follow. This is not what "Lordship" looks like.

Obedience is when God leads and we follow, and this is the way that it should be. In the previous examples of Noah and Abraham, you will notice that God called them first, they did not dream up these things; God called on them, they believed God, and then they obediently did what God asked of them.

Examples of wrong motives are when we do good works to gain God's favor or to earn God's approval, or even to earn our salvation? If so then these things are meaningless because God already loves us dearly. It is even worse if we are doing these things to gain the approval of men. These "dead works" are self-seeking of glory for ourselves, for the good things that we have done.

Jesus said to his disciples:

> Not all people who sound religious are really godly. They may refer to me as "Lord," but they still won't enter the Kingdom of Heaven. The decisive issue is whether they obey my Father in heaven. On judgment day many will tell me, "Lord, Lord, we prophesied in your name and cast out demons in your name and performed many miracles in your name." But I will reply, "I never knew you. Go away, the things you did were unauthorized."
>
> Matthew 7:21–23 (NLT)

In this scripture we see that these religious-looking people are doing "good deeds." They are performing miracles, prophesying and casting out demons. And they believe, because they are doing them in Jesus' name. Yet they will not be going to heaven. We see that the *decisive issue is whether they obey God*, then they are doing things that God has called them to do, or authorized them to do, instead of what they have "dreamed up" themselves.

What Jesus says to me through these verses is: *"There are many people doing all kinds of great works in my name, but very few who are doing what I have called them to do."*

Only when we put our faith in Jesus Christ to make us right with God, because of His sacrifice on the cross for the forgiveness of our sins, have we truly accepted Jesus as our Savior. But when we repent of our sins and vow to follow Jesus and His teachings, then Jesus becomes our LORD. Furthermore, it is only when we surrender our will to follow God's will that He becomes our LORD. And it is when we let God lead, by waiting for His calling, and then through obedience we do all that God has asked us to do, that God becomes our LORD.

Jesus wants to be both our Savior and LORD. In other words, it's trust and obey—trust Him as our Savior, and obey Him as LORD.

If we have really asked Jesus to be LORD of our life, then obedience should follow. Jesus proclaimed, "Why do you call me, 'LORD, LORD,' and do not do what I say?" (Luke 6:46, NIV).

If we call Jesus "LORD," then we need to let Him be LORD. We need to let Jesus lead, and we need to follow.

Another way to look at what God means by LORDship, involves sacrificial living; where we *die to self, so that we can live for Christ.*

This sacrificial living does not mean that we need to sacrifice things such as offerings of animals. And it does not mean we need to celebrate certain holy days, or practice forms of self-denial.

God says in Isaiah:

> "To what purpose *is* the multitude of your sacrifices to Me?" says the Lord.
>
> "I have had enough of burnt offerings of rams and the fat of fed cattle. I do not delight in the blood of bulls, or of lambs or goats. When you come to appear before Me, who has required this from your hand, to trample My courts?
>
> Bring no more futile sacrifices; incense is an abomination to Me. The New Moons, the Sabbaths, and the calling of assemblies—I cannot endure iniquity and the sacred meeting. Your New Moons and your appointed feasts, My soul hates; they are a trouble to Me, I am weary of bearing them.
>
> When you spread out your hands, I will hide My eyes from you; even though you make many prayers, I will not hear. Your hands are full of blood.
>
> Wash yourselves, make yourselves clean; put away the evil of your doings from before My eyes. Cease to do evil, learn to do good; seek justice,

rebuke the oppressor; defend the fatherless, plead for the widow.

Isaiah 1:11–17 (NKJV)

God wants no more of these kinds of sacrifices. The days of sacrificing animals is done. The burning of incense, holy days of obligation, and the celebrations of the festivals established under The Law are all part of the old covenant, which is no longer in effect. God doesn't want us making ritualistic sacrifices, while we continue practicing sinful ways.

> So don't let anyone condemn you for what you eat or drink, or for not celebrating certain holy days or new moon ceremonies or Sabbaths. For these rules are only shadows of the reality yet to come. And Christ himself is that reality. Don't let anyone condemn you by insisting on pious self-denial or the worship of angels, saying they have had visions about these things. Their sinful minds have made them proud, and they are not connected to Christ, the head of the body. For he holds the whole body together with its joints and ligaments, and it grows as God nourishes it.
>
> You have died with Christ, and he has set you free from the spiritual powers of this world. So why do you keep on following the rules of the world, such as, "Don't handle! Don't taste! Don't touch!" Such rules are mere human teachings about things that deteriorate as soon as we use them. These rules may seem wise because they require strong devotion, pious self-denial, and

> severe bodily discipline. But they provide no help in conquering a person's evil desires.
>
> Colossians 2:16–23 (NLT)

What we eat or drink, or don't eat or drink, doesn't matter to God. For example: Giving up meat on Fridays is not what God wants. Mandatory "holy days of obligation," where we *have* to go to church, are not important.

All these things lead to self-reliance, self-righteousness and pride toward the things that we have done. Though these things seem like they would lead to godliness, they actually have a negative effect. They lead to pride in what we have done to save ourselves, and away from trusting in Jesus' sacrifice on the cross to save us. They diminish our need for a Savior.

All these ritualistic-type sacrifices were only a shadow of the kind of sacrifices that please God; just as the sacrificial lamb given to cover the sins of men, was only a shadow of things to come—the sacrifice of the "Lamb of God" (Jesus Christ), for the forgiveness of sins.

What God wants from each of us now, is to be living sacrifices:

> And so, dear brothers and sisters, I plead with you to give your bodies to God because of all he has done for you. Let them be a living and holy sacrifice—the kind he will find acceptable. This is truly the way to worship him."
>
> Romans 12:1 (NLT)

It's by submitting to God's will, rather than following our own agenda, or it's when we get to the point where we *die to self, so that Christ can live in us*, that God is then able to accomplish His work through us.

We need to come to the mind-set described in Galatians: "I have been crucified with Christ; it is no longer I who live, but Christ lives in me; and the *life* which I now live in the flesh I live by faith in the Son of God, who loved me and gave Himself for me" (Galatians 2:20, NKJV).

Just as Christ sacrificed himself for us, now God wants us to offer ourselves back to Him. What I mean by this is to give up *our* agenda, *our* wants, *our* desires and *our* will, for God's will. Then we are truly living for God! When we give of our time, money and resources to help others or to do God's work that He has asked us to do, these are pleasing to God.

Lots of times, God's agenda is in conflict with our agenda—the things that God calls us to do will come as interruptions. Like when a friend calls and needs a listening ear, or when someone asks for our help. At times like these, God wants us to put aside our agenda and be a part of his work.

I was once in London, England with a tour group. We came upon a young girl that was playing a musical instrument, in hopes of getting some contributions. She was obviously a person that lived on the streets—begging for money to survive.

I sat down beside her and started talking to her about her needs. She was sick, and she said she was trying to get enough money so she could get off the street for the night and find a room to sleep in.

Just then my wife, Julie, who was walking with a cane, because of an injury to her hip, said, "Let's get going; my leg really hurts."

I was torn between whether I should do something to help this girl, or if I should take care of my wife.

I should have quickly given the girl enough money for a room, and then left with my wife. But instead I just left.

I started feeling guilty about not helping this girl; so after helping Julie get back to our room, I told Julie that I was going back to help her.

As I walked down the street, I noticed that every beggar that we had come across on our way to the hotel now had someone helping them, even the girl that I was returning to help.

Then God told me, "I don't need you to help Me with My work-I can find somebody else to do it."

Then I realized: It should not be considered a chore or a burden to help God with his work it should be considered a privilege. Because when we join God in His work, we get to experience God, as He does His work through us.

The reason that God calls us to do certain things is because God expects Christians to "bear fruit."

Jesus says, "This is to my Father's glory, that you bear much fruit, showing yourselves to be my disciples (John 15:8, NIV).

This *fruit* is drawing others to Christ by our witness.

You see this in "The Parable of the Farmer Scattering Seed." "The good soil represents the hearts of those who truly accept God's message and produce a huge harvest-thirty, sixty or even a hundred times as much as had been planted" (Matthew 13:23, NLT).

You also see this theme demonstrated in "The Parable of the Talents":

Again, it will be like a man going on a journey, who called his servants and entrusted his property to them. To one he gave five talents of money, to another two talents, and to another one talent, each according to his ability. Then he went on his journey. The man who had received the five talents went at once and put his money to work and gained five more. So also, the one with the two talents gained two more. But the man who had received the one talent went off, dug a hole in the ground and hid his master's money.

After a long time the master of those servants returned and settled accounts with them. The man who had received the five talents brought the other five. "Master," he said, "you entrusted me with five talents. See, I have gained five more."

His master replied, "Well done, good and faithful servant! You have been faithful with a few things; I will put you in charge of many things. Come and share your master's happiness!"

The man with the two talents also came. "Master," he said, "you entrusted me with two talents; see, I have gained two more."

His master replied, "Well done, good and faithful servant! You have been faithful with a few things; I will put you in charge of many things. Come and share your master's happiness!"

Then the man who had received the one talent came. "Master," he said, "I knew that you are a hard man, harvesting where you have not sown and gathering where you have not scattered seed. So I was afraid and went out and hid your talent in the ground. See, here is what belongs to you."

His master replied, "You wicked, lazy servant! So you knew that I harvest where I have not sown and gather where I have not scattered seed? Well then, you should have put my money on deposit with the bankers, so that when I returned I would have received it back with interest.

Take the talent from him and give it to the one who has the ten talents. For everyone who has will be given more, and he will have an abundance. Whoever does not have, even what he has will be taken from him. And throw that worthless servant outside, into the darkness, where there will be weeping and gnashing of teeth."

Matthew 25:14–30 (NIV)

So you see, God doesn't want us to just be satisfied with our own salvation, He wants us to use the talents and spiritual gifts that He has given us to witness to others about Him.

Here are a couple examples of how God rewarded me for being obedient to his calling to bear fruit … fruit that will last.

It was the summer of 1999, when my daughter, Kayla Jo, accepted Jesus Christ as her Lord and Savior.

Earlier that summer, Kayla asked me if I could take her to a youth rally in Fargo, ND for her 13th birthday. She wanted our whole family to go along.

I do crop dusting for a living (I spray farmer's fields with an airplane). I am extremely busy in the summer; I work every day. So when Kayla came to me with this request, I said that I would have to think about it and get back to her (actually, I needed to pray about it).

After praying, I knew that this was something that God wanted me to do; I remember praying to God, "If this is going to happen, it will have to come from you" because I knew that taking a day off was very difficult, but Kayla wanted me to take the entire weekend off (Friday afternoon to Sunday afternoon). This was going to take a miracle!

On the day that we were to leave for Fargo, my hired pilot, Kyle, and I were both spraying and rain clouds were building all around us. As the time to leave came, it started to rain; I put the airplane in the hangar, jumped in the car and we were off. It rained the entire weekend, and I would not have been able to do any work anyway; so God did take care of everything!

The rally was awesome! The band *Mercy Me* was leading worship, and Mark Matlock was teaching Saturday evening (on Kayla's birthday). Mark was talking about the message from Revelation 20; he was saying that when a person accepts Jesus Christ as their Lord and Savior, their names are written in the "Book of Life," and anyone's name that is in the "Book of Life" will live forever with God, and those whose names are not written in the "Book of Life" will be thrown into the "Lake of Fire."

Kayla leaned over and whispered in my ear, "Dad, that is so easy."

I replied, "Yeah, that's the amazing thing about God's love; He made it that easy. But, it wasn't easy for Jesus to die on the cross so that our sins could be forgiven."

At that moment, Kayla broke down and started weeping as the full impact of this realization hit home. At this same time, I was looking into Kayla's eyes, and I saw the "Light of Christ" enter her, and I felt the Holy Spirit as He swept over her.

Jesus said, "Just as you can hear the wind but can't tell where it comes from or where it is going, so you can't explain how people are born of the Spirit" (John 3:8, NLT).

I looked over at my youngest son, Jared (who was dancing in the aisles to the music just moments before, but was now weeping), as the Holy Spirit swept over him too. Shortly after this, there was an invitation to formally accept Jesus as LORD and Savior. Both Kayla and Jared went down to do this, but I knew that in their hearts, it was already done.

This experience really showed me the importance of obedience to God. I could have told Kayla that there was no way that I could take the weekend off of work and take her to this event, but because I was obedient to God and brought her, God saved both Kayla and Jared that weekend.

Looking back, I wouldn't have traded this day for anything in the whole world. I can't tell you the peace in your heart that comes with knowing that your children are going to spend eternity with you (and God), in heaven.

A few years later, I was at a youth rally called *Acquire the Fire*, with a group of kids from our church. I was just sitting back, taking it all in, when all of a sudden my heart started racing. I thought, *What is happening to me?*

Then God began to speak to my heart. I didn't hear a voice, but I knew that it was God and I knew what God wanted me to do. He wanted me to witness to a girl that was in our group named Luisa. She was a foreign exchange student from Germany. Her host family went to our church, and so she was with our youth group.

I turned to see where she was sitting, and I said to God, "But she is sitting six seats away. How am I supposed to witness to her?"

Then God told me what to say to her. Again, I did not hear a voice—I just knew what it was that He wanted me to tell her.

I thought, *Okay, I have to do this—but how?*

The session was just coming to an end, and then we were going to leave for a half-hour intermission. I knew that I was not going to be able to witness to her until we returned from the break. So I planned to try to get seated next to her upon our return.

I got there early and chose a seat next to the one Luisa had been sitting in. I sat down, and shortly afterward, Luisa returned. She gave me a funny look when she saw me sitting there, but came over and sat next to me.

I had a pocket full of chocolates; I offered her one and struck up a conversation with her. She was in the senior high Sunday school class that I taught, but I never got a chance to talk to her about her faith. So I took advantage of this time by doing so.

"Luisa, I have never gotten a chance to ask you about your faith. Do you believe in God?" I inquired.

She said that she believed God was like an energy, or aura.

I asked if she believed in evolution, or if she believed the world was created by God?

She said she believed in evolution.

I asked her if she believed in heaven and hell, and what did she believe would happen to her when she died?

She said that she believed in reincarnation (that you come back to earth to live another life).

This whole time, I was not saying too much and I was not arguing with her about what she believed; I was just listening.

We talked about many things as the program continued with videos of teens that had accepted Christ into their hearts, and their testimonies of how Christ had transformed their lives because of what Christ was doing in them and through them.

Then it came to the time when the leader of the program gave an altar call (this is where he asks anyone who would like to accept Jesus as their Lord and Savior, to come down toward the front, and he would help lead them in a prayer to ask Jesus into their hearts).

As a thousand or more kids came forward, I asked Luisa, "What do you think of all this; do you think these people are really experiencing something, or are they just faking it?"

She kind of shrugged her shoulders and said, "I don't know."

As she was pondering this question, I decided now was the time to say to her what God told me to say. I looked Luisa in the eyes, and I asked, *"Luisa, would you like to know God?"*

She looked at me meekly, shrugged her shoulders, and said, "I don't know."

Then I continued with more of what God told me to say: *"Luisa, you are not here by accident, God has called you here by name."*

She looked up at me again, and was really focusing on what I was saying.

Then I went on, "*He stands at the door to your heart and knocks, but you have to let Him in!*"

Just as I got the last words out of my mouth, that God told me to say, I heard, "Ken!"

I turned around. It was my wife, Julie. I asked, "What?"

She said, "Jared (our youngest son), is going down to accept Christ. You need to go down with him."

I said, "But I'm witnessing to Luisa. You go down with Jared."

She said, "You are better at this than me. You go down with him."

I knew that Jared had already accepted Christ three years earlier, when he was just nine years old. I didn't understand what was happening, but I knew that my son needed me to go down to pray with him (Jared told me later that he didn't understand what he was doing the first time, but he did now). I went thinking, "I am going to lose Luisa."

I know that it was very meaningful to Jared, and that he really appreciated that I went down with him for support, and I was glad that I could be there for him, but I kept thinking about Luisa as well.

When we were done praying, we went back to our seats. To my surprise, Luisa was not there. I asked Julie where she was.

She told me that after I left, Abby (one of Luisa's host sisters, who is a dynamite witness for Christ, who had been witnessing to Luisa at home, and who had been praying for Luisa for some time), turned around and saw that Luisa was in tears (as the Holy Spirit was at work in her heart), and asked her, "If you would like to go down and accept Jesus into your heart, I'll go with you."

Then a student next to Abby stood up and said, "I'll go with you, too."

Then, three more students stood up and said they would go too.

Luisa had just been telling me how alienated she felt, not being a Christian. She felt that she didn't have any friends that cared about her. How wonderful it was that these kids were now reaching out to her.

Luisa accepted their offer, and all of them went down with Luisa and prayed with her as she accepted Jesus into her heart.

Just as Julie finished telling me this, Luisa and the others returned to their seats. I looked at Abby, who was grinning from ear to ear; she gave me a two-thumbs up. I gave her the same sign back, and knew exactly what had happened. Abby had picked up right where I had left off with Luisa. It was so amazing to think that God had used me to get Luisa to a certain point, and then had also used Abby and these kids to finish the work that God was doing.

I looked up at Luisa as she approached her seat, and I asked her, "Did you go down and accept Jesus into your heart?"

She looked at me with a big, bright smile and exclaimed, "Yes!"

I reached out and gave her a big hug.

As the program continued, I could tell that Luisa was in deep thought, as the impact of what had just happened settled into her heart. She looked somewhat dazed, shocked, and a little scared.

I don't know today if Luisa is still following Jesus, but I could tell in the months that followed, before she returned to Germany, that she had a sparkle in her eye that was not there before. It was the "Light of Christ" shining through.

I realized from this experience that while I was being

obedient to God in witnessing to Luisa, God was busy working in Jared's heart as well, and partially due to my obedience to God's calling, but mostly due to God, both Jared and Luisa made commitments to Christ. I was also blessed, because I was able to experience God as He did this through me. I stayed connected to God and He to me, and together we produced fruit, as two more were added to the Kingdom of God.

Still, our greatest witness of Jesus Christ is by the way we live our lives. Because Christ lives in us, we can be living examples to others by being a "light" that shines out in this dark world. The reason God doesn't take us directly to heaven to be with Him after we have accepted Jesus as our LORD and Savior is because He wants us to be a witness to others. This witness can draw people closer to God. But we must be careful that we are not a negative witness to others, because this will cause them to move further away from God. We must be wary of hypocrisy—where we say one thing and then do another, or say we are Christians, but don't act very godly; this would certainly not be to our advantage.

> You are the light of the world. A city that is set on a hill cannot be hidden. Nor do they light a lamp and put it under a basket, but on a lampstand, and it gives light to all *who are* in the house. Let your light so shine before men, that they may see your good works and glorify your Father in heaven.
>
> Matthew 5:14–16 (NKJV)

Jesus says in the Gospel of John, "Whoever has my commands and obeys them, he is the one who loves me. He who loves me will be loved by my Father, and I too will love him and show myself to him" (John 14:21, NIV).

Again, Jesus says, "As the Father has loved me, so have I loved you. Now remain in my love. If you obey my commands, you will remain in my love, just as I have obeyed my Father's commands and remain in his love" (John 15:9–10, NIV).

So once more, we see the importance of obedience. When we obey God we remain in His love.

Another thing that God showed me as I sought the truth about salvation is that walking in obedience to God is not just about one choice; it is a life journey of choices. Each day we must make the choice to follow Jesus. In fact, with each decision that we make, we must choose if we are going to follow God's way or the world's way (or even our own way).

I have seen many people make a one-time decision to follow Christ, but then continue to live their life the same way that they always have. They must think, "Okay, I have asked Jesus into my heart; I have my ticket to heaven, so now I can do whatever I want."

When we become a Christian, God calls us out of the world. We are no longer supposed to take part in the things of the world. We are not to be conformed to the ways of the world, but to be transformed through the renewing of our minds, by the power of the Holy Spirit, who now lives in us.

"Do not conform any longer to the pattern of this world, but be transformed by the renewing of your mind. Then you will be able to test and approve what God's will is—his good, pleasing and perfect will" (Romans 12:2, NIV).

When we become a Christian, we are to take off our old self, and put on our new self. We are to become a new creation, through Christ Jesus, our LORD.

> You were taught, with regard to your former way of life, to put off your old self, which is being corrupted by its deceitful desires; to be made new in the attitude of your minds; and to put on the new self, created to be like God in true righteousness and holiness.
>
> Ephesians 4:22–24 (NIV)

And it is the Holy Spirit who guides us into this new way of living.

Not that we have to become a "good person" in order to become a follower of Christ. No—Jesus accepts us just as we are, but then the Holy Spirit should begin His work in our lives, leading us to become this new, born-again person that God has called us to be. We should begin striving to become more Christ-like, as we draw closer to Him.

One thing that we cannot do—we cannot live with one foot in each world. We cannot be a follower of Christ, and live our lives the way that the world does.

Jesus gave this message to the Apostle John, for the Church in Laodicea, "I know your deeds, that you are neither cold nor hot. I wish you were either one or the other! So, because you are lukewarm—neither hot nor cold—I am about to spit you out of my mouth!" (Revelation 3:15–16, NIV).

Jesus is saying, because we are trying to live our life with one foot in each world (I call this: "sitting on the fence"), He will reject us.

And James says, "You adulterous people, don't you know that friendship with the world is hatred toward God? Anyone who chooses to be a friend of the world becomes an enemy of God" (James 4:4, NIV).

James is referring to people who try to live their life with one foot in each world, when he exclaims, you adulterers—it's because of their unfaithfulness. They are like a man that does not stay devoted to one woman in marriage. God wants us to be faithful to Him alone, and not have, "the world and its ways," as our mistress.

> Do not love the world or anything in the world. If anyone loves the world, the love of the Father is not in him. For everything in the world—the cravings of sinful man, the lust of his eyes and the boasting of what he has and does—comes not from the Father but from the world. The world and its desires pass away, but the man who does the will of God lives forever.
>
> 1 John 2:15–17 (NIV)

I would like you to look at what Jesus says in these verses, "If the world hates you, keep in mind that it hated me first. If you belonged to the world, it would love you as its own. As it is, you do not belong to the world, but I have chosen you out of the world. That is why the world hates you" (John 15:18–19, NIV).

Jesus is telling us that we will face persecution from the world because of our allegiance to Him. It's because we no longer belong to this world when we accept Christ as our Lord and Savior; we now belong to the Kingdom of God.

Another reason that we cannot be friends to both God and this world, is because we live in a fallen world—a world corrupted by the lies and schemes of Satan.

"We know that we are children of God, and that the whole world is under the control of the evil one" (1 John 5:19, NIV).

The Book of Revelation tells us how this is:

> And war broke out in heaven: Michael and his angels fought with the dragon; and the dragon and his angels fought, but they did not prevail, nor was a place found for them in heaven any longer. So the great dragon was cast out, that serpent of old, called the Devil and Satan, who deceives the whole world; he was cast to the earth, and his angels were cast out with him.
>
> Then I heard a loud voice saying in heaven, "Now salvation, and strength, and the kingdom of our God, and the power of His Christ have come, for the accuser of our brethren, who accused them before our God day and night, has been cast down. And they overcame him by the blood of the Lamb and by the word of their testimony, and they did not love their lives to the death. Therefore rejoice, O heavens, and you who dwell in them! Woe to the inhabitants of the earth and the sea! For the devil has come down to you, having great wrath, because he knows that he has a short time."
>
> Revelation 12:7–12 (NKJV)

Jesus even referred to Satan as the prince of this world, "The time of judgment for the world has come, when the prince of this world will be cast out" (John 12:31, NLT).

Yes, we live in a fallen world, polluted by the deceptions of Satan. Ever since Adam and Eve were deceived by Satan and took that first bite of forbidden fruit, we have been separated from God by our sins and our transgressions.

We are born with a sinful nature; nobody has to teach us how to sin, it comes quite naturally. When we are young we think that the world revolves around us; we want everything our own way. We start to listen to the lies of Satan, who is the "prince of this world," and we start to follow the ways of the world, rather than the ways of God.

And now that we have become followers of God, we cannot continue to live our lives in this same way!

I find that the ways of the world are almost always the opposite of God's ways. Some examples of these look like this:

The World's Way	God's Way
Look out for number 1, self.	First love God, then others, and then self.
If it feels good, do it.	Not everything is good for your soul.
Success = power, wealth	The first will be last; the greatest in God's kingdom will be the servant of all.
Take revenge yourself.	Forgiveness, leave vengeance to God.
Hate your enemies	Love your enemies.
Seek glory for yourself.	Give God the glory.
Pride.	Humility.
Divorce and adultery are okay.	Remain loyal to your spouse.
Pre-marital sex is okay.	Sex is to be saved for marriage
Homosexuality is okay.	Marriage is between one man and one woman.

These are just a few examples; this list could go on and on. That is why James says that to be a friend of this world, makes us an enemy of God, and that is why we cannot live with one foot in each world. We must choose to follow one or the other, because they are opposite directions (as far as the east is from the west).

So, does this mean that God hates the world?

No—in fact the Gospel of John says, "For God so loved the world, that he sent his one and only Son, so that everyone who believes in him would not perish but have eternal life" (John 3:16, NIV).

And the very next verse says, "For God did not send his Son into the world to condemn the world, but to save the world through him" (John 3:17, NIV).

Jesus was sent into this world to save those who put their faith in Him.

The Scriptures say, "Enter by the narrow gate; for wide *is* the gate and broad *is* the way that leads to destruction, and there are many who go in by it. Because narrow *is* the gate and difficult *is* the way which leads to life, and there are few who find it" (Matthew 7:13–14, NKJV).

I urge you to search for the road that leads to God, by following His ways and not the ways of the world.

Do not cling to this world or the things in it, for Jesus says, "Anyone who loves their life in this world will lose their life in God's kingdom; and what good would it do for you to gain the whole world, but lose your own soul in the process. Is anything more valuable than your soul?" (Matthew 16:25–26)

So, again I tell you, following Christ is about every choice that comes our way; we must decide, are we going to follow God in obedience or are we going to follow "the world"?

Some of the things that God calls us to do are individual things that are unique for that person.

Examples of these would be: for Noah to build a boat; for Abraham to leave his country; for Moses to lead God's people out of Egypt. For Paul it was to preach to the Gentiles. For you, it may be that God is calling you to be a good mother or father to your children, to teach a Bible study, or to go on a missionary trip.

There are some things that God expects all Christians to do. "Learn to do good. Seek justice. Help the oppressed. Defend the orphan. Fight for the rights of widows" (Isaiah 1:17). Other things might be to help the poor by feeding the hungry and providing shelter and clothing for those in need. If we want to walk in obedience to God, we must all do these things.

And for the individual things God calls us to do we must seek God as though we are on a quest. We must find our destiny (the person that God has created us to be, doing the things that God has called us to do). And God has a plan and a purpose for each one of us. It's up to us to find out what this is.

The only way to know what God is calling us to do is to know God. We must have a personal relationship with God which is what we will look at in the next chapter.

Knowing God

In this chapter we will take a look at the importance of knowing God, and how to have a personal relationship with Him.

Recall the example of the life of Noah that I used previously: Noah had a close relationship with God, Noah believed God when He told Noah to build a boat, because He was going to send a flood upon the earth, and Noah was obedient and built a boat, and it saved him and his household (Genesis 6:9–22).

So, would it do you or me any good to build a boat? Would that save us?

No, because if we know God and know The Scriptures, we know that God promised to never send another flood upon the whole earth (Genesis 9:11–16). And that is not what God has called us to do.

We see by this example that we cannot duplicate somebody else's calling from God and expect it to have the same outcome. We each have a unique calling that we must wait for God to reveal to us.

I have seen times when people interfere with God's work when they do ministry that God has not called them to do.

By doing this, they are not letting the person God *has* called into that position, to accomplish their task. This is a grave mistake, and the ministry will suffer because of this. Little or no fruit will be produced, and everyone involved will feel burdened, disappointed, and discouraged. Nobody should take over someone else's calling from God; we must seek from God our own calling.

But how do we know what God has called us to do? There is only one way: we need to know God!

In Matthew 7:21–23, Jesus was telling his disciples about some religious-looking people who were not going to get into the Kingdom of God. Even though these people in verses 21 and 22 were doing great works in Jesus' name, Jesus still told them to go away, because He never knew them.

But I will reply, "I never knew you. Go away; the things you did were unauthorized" (Matthew 7:23, NLT).

We also see this in the parable of the Ten Bridesmaids:

> At that time the kingdom of heaven will be like ten virgins who took their lamps and went out to meet the bridegroom. Five of them were foolish and five were wise. The foolish ones took their lamps but did not take any oil with them. The wise, however, took oil in jars along with their lamps. The bridegroom was a long time in coming, and they all became drowsy and fell asleep.
>
> At midnight the cry rang out: "Here's the bridegroom! Come out to meet him!"
>
> Then all the virgins woke up and trimmed their

lamps. The foolish ones said to the wise, "Give us some of your oil; our lamps are going out."

"No," they replied. "There may not be enough for both us and you. Instead, go to those who sell oil and buy some for yourselves."

But while they were on their way to buy the oil, the bridegroom arrived. The virgins who were ready went in with him to the wedding banquet. And the door was shut.

Later the others also came. "Sir! Sir!" they said. "Open the door for us!"

But he replied, "I tell you the truth, I don't know you."

Matthew 25:1–12 (NIV)

This parable points out the importance of being ready for Christ's return as well as that of getting to know Him now while there is still time, before it is too late, because none of us knows the time of His return or how much longer we have on this earth.

We must have a personal relationship with God, or we will never know the things that God has called us to do. It may seem that we are doing good things in the name of Jesus, but we will not be doing the things that God created us to do, or to be all that God has created us to be.

Jesus says more about the importance of this personal relationship with God in these verses:

> I am the vine; you are the branches. If a man remains in me and I in him, he will bear much fruit; apart from me you can do nothing. If anyone does not remain in me, he is like a branch that is thrown away and withers; such branches are picked up, thrown into the fire and burned. If you remain in me and my words remain in you, ask whatever you wish, and it will be given you. This is to my Father's glory, that you bear much fruit, showing yourselves to be my disciples.
>
> John 15:5–8 (NIV)

We must stay joined to Jesus, and we must be able to communicate with God so that we will know what His will is for our life. In order to communicate with God, we need to be able to recognize His voice.

> I tell you the truth, the man who does not enter the sheep pen by the gate, but climbs in by some other way, is a thief and a robber. The man who enters by the gate is the shepherd of his sheep. The watchman opens the gate for him, and the sheep listen to his voice. He calls his own sheep by name and leads them out. When he has brought out all his own, he goes on ahead of them, and his sheep follow him because they know his voice. But they will never follow a stranger; in fact, they will run away from him because they do not recognize a stranger's voice.
>
> John 10:1–5 (NIV)

> I am the good shepherd; I know my sheep and my sheep know me—just as the Father knows me and I know the Father—and I lay down my life for the sheep. I have other sheep that are not of this sheep pen. I must bring them also. They too will listen to my voice, and there shall be one flock and one shepherd.
>
> John 10:14–16 (NIV)

"My sheep listen to my voice; I know them, and they follow me" (John 10:27, NIV).

These verses clearly tell us that if we are to be followers of Christ, "The Good Shepherd," we need to recognize his voice, then, we will truly know Him.

The reason we need to recognize His voice is because Satan can also speak to us, and we need to know the difference, or we will be following the wrong voice.

Satan speaks to us, either directly, or through the many voices of the world that call out to us, trying to lure us away from God. The world is full of "false messiahs," (things that seem important, but are really just trying to steal us away from our relationship with God). In fact, one of Satan's greatest tools is to keep us so busy and wrapped up in the world that we have no time for God.

I think that it would be helpful here to look at the history of how God speaks to His people throughout The Bible. So let's start at the beginning, when God created the heavens and the earth, and everything in them. God created man to be with Him and to fellowship with Him in a love relationship, but then as is shown in Genesis 3, sin entered into the world and separated us from God. In the beginning God spoke directly to Adam, but after Adam and Eve sinned they hid from God and were ashamed. Then God punished Adam and Eve for their sin and banished them from the Garden of Eden.

Their offspring continued in sin, as their son Cain murdered his brother Abel.

Through the following generations men continued to become more and more wicked:

> Then the LORD saw that the wickedness of man was great in the earth, and that every intent of the thoughts of his heart was only evil continually. And the LORD was sorry that He had made man on the earth, and He was grieved in His heart. So the LORD said, "I will destroy man whom I have created from the face of the earth, both man and beast, creeping thing and birds of the air, for I am sorry that I have made them."
>
> Genesis 6:5–7 (NKJV)

However, God still had close relationships with certain righteous men, such as Enoch: "He enjoyed a close relationship with God throughout his life. Then suddenly, he disappeared because God took him" (Genesis 5:24, NLT).

"It was by faith that Enoch was taken up to heaven without dying–'suddenly he disappeared because God took him.' But before he was taken up, he was approved as pleasing to God" (Hebrews 11:5, NLT).

"A man named Noah was also a righteous and blameless man who consistently followed God's will and enjoyed a close relationship with God" (Genesis 6:9, NLT).

As we see in the next few chapters of Genesis, God

destroyed the inhabitants of the earth with a great flood, and only Noah and his family, and a pair of each living creature survived on a ship that Noah built according to God's instructions.

Many generations passed after the flood, and again God found favor with a man named Abram (Genesis 12–25), and again God spoke face to face with Abram, who God renamed Abraham, which means "the father of many," because God was about to bless Abraham's offspring as His own "chosen people."

This blessing passed down to Abraham's son Isaac, and on to Isaac's son Jacob, who God renamed Israel. Israel had twelve sons who became known as the twelve tribes of Israel. Jacob and his sons lived in the land that God had promised to Abraham and his offspring, the land of Canaan, which later became the country of Israel.

Jacob also had a son named Joseph, who was sold into slavery by his brothers and was brought to the land of Egypt. Joseph found favor with Pharaoh, who made him the second highest ruler in Egypt. God had given the Pharaoh a dream that Joseph had interpreted as seven years of plenty followed by seven years of famine. Joseph led the Egyptians to save grain in the years of plenty to store up for the coming seven years of drought. When the drought came, the land of Canaan was also without food, and Jacob sent his sons to find food in Egypt. They were reconciled with their brother Joseph and all of Jacob's family moved to the land of Egypt.

Several generations passed and the Israelites became slaves of the Egyptians and were forced into hard labor. The Israelites called out to God, and God heard their prayers and spoke to Moses from a burning bush and later face-to-face. God sent Moses to rescue "His chosen people" and return them to the land that God had promised them through Abraham.

God sent plagues against the Egyptians, until Pharaoh finally agreed to let the Israelites go. But Pharaoh became angry and chased after the Israelites and cornered them against the Red Sea. Then God miraculously divided the Red Sea so that the Israelites could escape on dry ground to the other side. Pharaoh and his army chased after the Israelites, but after the Israelites were safely on the other side, God closed the sea once again and all of Pharaoh's army was destroyed.

Two months later God revealed himself at Mt. Sinai (Exodus 19 and 20), in a powerful display of smoke and fire that shook the whole mountain.

> When the people heard the thunder and the loud blast of the horn, and when they saw the lightning and the smoke billowing from the mountain, they stood at a distance, trembling with fear. And they said to Moses, "You tell us what God says, and we will listen. But don't let God speak directly to us. If he does we will die!"
>
> Exodus 20:18–19 (NLT)

So this began the time of the Judges, where God spoke to His people through the Judges, (these were people that God appointed to lead his people), starting with Moses and ending with Samuel.

Then in (1Samuel 8), the Israelites requested from God, a king, to govern them. This upset God, but God gave into the peoples' request by giving them a king.

During the reign of kings in Israel, God spoke through the prophets (which were men anointed by God to be His spokesmen to the people). One of the great prophets of this time was Elijah.

Because the people of Israel were trying to kill him, Elijah fled to the mountains.

The LORD came to Elijah and said:

> Go out and stand before me on the mountain. And as Elijah stood there, the LORD passed by, and a mighty windstorm hit the mountain. It was such a terrible blast that the rocks were torn loose, but the LORD was not in the wind. After the wind there was an earthquake, but the LORD was not in the earthquake. And after the earthquake there was a fire, but the LORD was not in the fire. And after the fire there was the sound of a gentle whisper.
>
> 1 Kings 19:11–12 (NLT)

Many times the voice of the LORD is a gentle whisper and if we are not listening intently, we will miss it.

Like Enoch, Elijah did not experience death, as "chariots of fire" came down from heaven and snatched Elijah up to heaven (2 Kings 2:11).

Through the time of the judges and the prophets, God's people were caught up in a vicious cycle of disobedience, which brought God's judgment against them, followed by a period of repentance, which brought peace and prosperity, until they rebelled once again.

Finally, after many repeated warnings from God, spoken through the prophets, God had enough of this and sent neighboring armies against Israel. These armies conquered Israel and those that survived were scattered into exile in foreign lands.

Also, through this period of time, God foretold through the prophets of a coming messiah that would rescue them and redeem them back to God. There were numerous signs, or prophecies that foretold many things about the Messiah, such as: where this messiah would be born, through what family lineage he would come from, how He would live, the purpose for which He came, and how He would die and after three days, would be resurrected.

The last message given by God during this time was through the prophet Malachi, or at least this is the last prophecy written in the Old Testament of the Holy Bible.

> Behold, I will send you Elijah the prophet Before the coming of the great and dreadful day of the Lord. And he will turn The hearts of the fathers to the children, And the hearts of the children to their fathers, Lest I come and strike the earth with a curse.
>
> Malachi 4:5–6 (NKJV)

Then there was a period of about four hundred years when God was silent, or at least there is a gap in the Holy Bible between the Old Testament and the New Testament of about this long.

During this time God brought many of the Israelites out of exile and back into their own land.

Then in fulfillment of the prophecy of Malachi, God sent an angel to a priest of the temple of God, named Zechariah, and told him that his wife, Elizabeth, would bear a son, *"with the spirit and power of Elijah, the prophet of old. He will precede the coming of the Lord, preparing the people for his arrival"* (Luke 1:17). They were to name him John (later known as John the Baptist).

God spoke through His prophets, and if they were truly a prophet of God, everything that they prophesied would come to pass just as God told them it would.

Here is an example of this: God spoke through Malachi about "the one" preceding the Messiah to be of the *spirit and power* of Elijah. Then God spoke through the prophet Zechariah, about how his son, John the Baptist, would be the fulfillment of this prophecy.

Jesus also confirmed this in the Gospel of Mark, "And they asked him, 'Why do the teachers of the law say that Elijah must come first?'" (Mark 9:11, NIV).

Jesus responded, "Elijah is indeed coming first to get everything ready. But I tell you, Elijah has already come, and they chose to abuse him, just as the Scriptures predicted" (Mark 9:13, NLT).

God continued to announce the coming of the Messiah through His angels:

> In the sixth month, God sent the angel Gabriel to Nazareth, a town in Galilee, to a virgin pledged to be married to a man named Joseph, a descendant of David. The virgin's name was Mary. The angel went to her and said, "Greetings, you who are highly favored! The LORD is with you."
>
> Mary was greatly troubled at his words and wondered what kind of greeting this might be. But the angel said to her, "Do not be afraid, Mary, you have found favor with God. You will be with child and give birth to a son, and you are to give him the name Jesus. He will be great and will be called the Son of the Most High. The LORD God will give him the throne of his

father David, and he will reign over the house of Jacob forever; his kingdom will never end."

"How will this be," Mary asked the angel, "since I am a virgin?"

The angel answered, "The Holy Spirit will come upon you, and the power of the Most High will overshadow you. So the holy one to be born will be called the Son of God. Even Elizabeth your relative is going to have a child in her old age, and she who was said to be barren is in her sixth month. For nothing is impossible with God."

"I am the Lord's servant," Mary answered. "May it be to me as you have said." Then the angel left her.

Luke 1:26–38 (NIV)

As you can see, God was about to fulfill all that He had promised through the prophets about the coming of the Lord; God was sending His own son to earth, The Promised One, The Messiah, The Savior of the World! And we see that God was speaking to people by sending messengers from heaven, the angels.

God continued to send more angels as they appeared to Joseph, the fiancé of Mary in Matthew 1:20, and again in 2:13, and again in 2:19.

God's angels appeared to the shepherds as they were watching their sheep on the night that Jesus was born, to announce the birth:

> Now there were in the same country shepherds living out in the fields, keeping watch over their flock by night. And behold, an angel of the LORD stood before them, and the glory of the LORD shone around them, and they were greatly afraid. Then the angel said to them, "Do not be afraid, for behold, I bring you good tidings of great joy which will be to all people. For there is born to you this day in the city of David a Savior, who is Christ the LORD. And this will be the sign to you: You will find a Babe wrapped in swaddling cloths, lying in a manger."
>
> And suddenly there was with the angel a multitude of the heavenly host praising God and saying:
>
> "Glory to God in the highest, And on earth peace, goodwill toward men!"
>
> Luke 2:8–14 (NKJV)

God used angels to speak to His people many times before, since the days of Abraham (Genesis 18), and several times to Daniel, as well as others, and God continues to send His messengers from time to time, including to myself, when God sent the "Angel of Truth" to me in a dream that I wrote about in chapter one.

The time was coming, in fact it was already here, when God would send His one and only Son into the world, and we know from the scriptures that Jesus is not only the Son of God, but the "Word of God" sent down to earth in the form of the Christ-child.

"In the beginning was the Word, and the Word was with God, and the Word was God" (John 1:1, NKJV).

"So the Word became human and lived here on earth among us. He was full of unfailing love and faithfulness. And we have seen his glory, the glory of the only Son of the Father" (John 1:14, NLT).

He is the "Bread of Life" talked about in John 6. And remember what Moses said: "People need more than bread for their life; real life comes by feeding on every word that comes from the mouth of God" (Deuteronomy 8:3, NLT).

Just as our physical bodies need food to sustain them, so our spirits need the "Word of God" to be sustained. Without this nourishment that comes from feeding on God's Word, our spirits become weak, and this will eventually end in the death of our souls. Our real strength comes from God.

Jesus says, "The true bread of God is the one who comes down from heaven and gives life to the world" (John 6:33, NLT).

"I am the Bread of Life. No one who comes to me will ever be hungry again. Those who believe in me will never thirst" (John 6:35, NLT).

"It is the Spirit who gives eternal life. Human effort accomplishes nothing. And the very words I have spoken to you are spirit and life" (John 6:63, NLT).

> The one who existed from the beginning is the one we have heard and seen. We saw him with our own eyes and touched him with our own hands. He is Jesus Christ, the Word of Life. This one who is life from God was shown to us, and we have seen him. And now we testify and announce to you that he is the one who is eternal life. He was with the Father, and then he

was shown to us. We are telling you about what we ourselves have actually seen and heard, so that you may have fellowship with us. And our fellowship is with the Father and with his Son, Jesus Christ.

1 John 1:1–3 (NLT)

While Jesus walked the earth, God spoke to His people through His Son, and these words are recorded in the books of Matthew, Mark, Luke and John, also known as the Gospels of the Holy Bible.

After Jesus' death, resurrection, and ascension into heaven, where He sits at the right hand of the Father, God sent the Holy Spirit to speak to His people.

Jesus said, "I will ask the Father, and he will give you another Counselor, who will never leave you. He is the Holy Spirit, who leads into all truth. The world at large cannot receive him, because it isn't looking for him and doesn't recognize him. But you do, because he lives with you now and later will be in you" (John 14:16–17, NLT).

"But when the Father sends the Counselor as my representative—and by the Counselor I mean the Holy Spirit—he will teach you everything and will remind you of everything I myself have told you" (John 14:26, NLT).

"But I will send you the Counselor—the Spirit of truth. He will come to you from the Father and will tell you all about me, and you must also tell others about me because you have been with me from the beginning" (John 15:26–27, NLT).

> When the Spirit of truth comes, he will guide you into all truth. He will not be presenting his own ideas; he will be telling you what he has heard. He will tell you about the future. He will

> bring me glory by revealing to you whatever he receives from me. All that the Father has is mine; this is what I mean when I say that the Spirit will reveal to you whatever he receives from me."
>
> John 16:13–15 (NLT)

> But we know these things because God has revealed them to us by his Spirit, and his Spirit searches out everything and shows us even God's deep secrets. No one can know what anyone else is really thinking except that person alone, and no one can know God's thoughts except God's own spirit. And God has actually given us his spirit (not the world's spirit), so we can know the wonderful things God has freely given us.
>
> 1 Corinthians 2:10–13 (NLT)

So now it is through the Holy Spirit that lives in us (when we become Christ's followers), and it is through the Word of God (the Holy Bible), that God speaks to His people.

When God speaks to me He often uses His Word (the scriptures of the Bible) to speak to me. Also, when God speaks to me, I do not hear an audible voice. God doesn't speak to my ears—he speaks to my heart, through the Holy Spirit. I know that it is God, and I know what He says.

As an example of this, in the summer of 2003, while flying my airplane over the crops of North-Central Minnesota, God began to speak to me about baptism.

For several weeks, I kept having the feeling that God wanted me to baptize Juliana Machado (the foreign exchange student from Brazil that had been living with us for the past eleven months). I had been sharing my faith with her and teaching her about God using scripture from the Holy Bible, since the day that she arrived. She accepted Jesus Christ as her LORD and Savior during her time with us, and now God was asking me to baptize her before sending her back to Brazil. I was having reservations about doing this. I felt that only ordained ministers were allowed to baptize; I didn't feel authorized, or qualified.

As I was pondering this in my mind, I said to God from my heart, "Who am I, that I should baptize Juliana?"

Then God began to speak to me. He used His words from the Holy Bible to speak to me, by reminding me of a story from the Book of Matthew. This takes place shortly after Jesus cleared the Temple of the moneychangers, by overturning their tables and chasing them out.

> Jesus entered the temple courts, and, while he was teaching, the chief priests and the elders of the people came to him. "By what authority are you doing these things?" they asked. "And who gave you this authority?"

> Jesus replied, "I will also ask you one question. If you answer me, I will tell you by what authority I am doing these things. John's baptism—where did it come from? Was it from heaven, or from men?"

> They discussed it among themselves and said, "If we say, 'From heaven,' he will ask, 'Then why didn't you believe him?' But if we say, 'From men'—we are afraid of the people, for they all hold that John was a prophet."

So they answered Jesus, "We don't know."

Then he said, "Neither will I tell you by what authority I am doing these things.

Matthew 21:23–27 (NIV)

Then God said to me, *"If baptism is of men, then men should authorize who can baptize. But if it is from God, shouldn't God be the one to authorize who can baptize?"*

I replied, "Yes LORD, but why me?"

Then God reminded me of the story of Philip and the Ethiopian eunuch from the Book of Acts:

> Now an angel of the LORD said to Philip, "Go south to the road—the desert road—that goes down from Jerusalem to Gaza." So he started out, and on his way he met an Ethiopian eunuch, an important official in charge of all the treasury of Candace, queen of the Ethiopians. This man had gone to Jerusalem to worship, and on his way home was sitting in his chariot reading the book of Isaiah the prophet. The Spirit told Philip, "Go to that chariot and stay near it."
>
> Then Philip ran up to the chariot and heard the man reading Isaiah the prophet. "Do you understand what you are reading?" Philip asked.
>
> "How can I," he said, "unless someone explains it to me?" So he invited Philip to come up and sit with him.

> The eunuch was reading this passage of Scripture: "He was led like a sheep to the slaughter, and as a lamb before the shearer is silent, so he did not open his mouth. In his humiliation he was deprived of justice. Who can speak of his descendants? For his life was taken from the earth."
>
> The eunuch asked Philip, "Tell me, please, who is the prophet talking about, himself or someone else?" Then Philip began with that very passage of Scripture and told him the good news about Jesus.
>
> As they traveled along the road, they came to some water and the eunuch said, "Look, here is water. Why shouldn't I be baptized?" And he gave orders to stop the chariot. Then both Philip and the eunuch went down into the water and Philip baptized him. When they came up out of the water, the Spirit of the Lord suddenly took Philip away, and the eunuch did not see him again, but went on his way rejoicing.
>
> Acts 8:26–39 (NIV)

Then God said to me, *"Just as Philip was the one to instruct the eunuch, and also was the one to baptize him, because you were the one to instruct Juliana, I want you to be the one to baptize her."*

What could I say but "Okay"?

I told Juliana what God said to me, and then I asked her if she wanted to be baptized. She said that she did.

So, on the Sunday before sending Juliana back to Brazil,

I got up early and asked God to show me what he wanted me to say and do. He gave me the instructions that I needed and I wrote down everything. So, after church, my family, some close friends and I took Juliana to the Crow Wing River to baptize her.

It was a very moving occasion. I really felt the presence of the Holy Spirit as we submerged Juliana under the water and baptized her. She is usually very squeamish, but she was so at peace, and you could feel that peacefulness radiate from her.

Afterwards, as we stood on the bank of the river, soaking wet, Juliana exclaimed that she felt so hot! I told her that was the presence of the Holy Spirit that she felt, because I often feel the same 'intense heat' when the Spirit works in me, or through me.

One more thing that God showed to me during this time from the Book of Matthew is when Jesus went to His disciples and said:

> All authority in heaven and on earth has been given to me. Therefore go and make disciples of all nations, baptizing them in the name of the Father and of the Son and of the Holy Spirit, and teaching them to obey everything I have commanded you. And surely I am with you always, to the very end of the age.
>
> Matthew 28:18–20 (NIV)

Then God showed me that Jesus did not go to the religious leaders of his time, and give them the authority to baptize and teach new disciples. He went to His disciples and authorized them to do this. And who are Jesus' disciples? They are all who believe in Him and follow Him.

Therefore, go and make disciples of all the nations, baptizing them...

God used the scriptures to teach me something new. I thought only ordained pastors could baptize, but God showed me that all of His disciples are authorized to baptize. The reason God was able to teach me this is because I knew the scriptures, so God was able to speak to me, through them. I knew that this was from God, because what He told me was in line with scripture, and God does not tell us things that contradict His Word, because the scriptures are the foundational truths of God.

Another time that God spoke to me using scripture was when my dogs Major and Tracker died.

In the fall of 2006 my hunting dog, Major, whom I had for nine years, died from cancer. He had not been feeling well for the last few months, and I had taken him to the vet several times. We did blood tests and x-rays and administered antibiotics, but nothing seemed to help.

Finally, I told the vet to open him up and see if he could find out what was wrong.

The vet called from the operating table and told me that Major was full of cancerous tumors, especially his liver. He said he could sew Major up and send him home, but he would experience lots of pain and suffering until he died.

After thinking it over I said, "You might as well not even wake him up." (I knew that Major was already suffering lots from this fatal disease.)

I had gotten another puppy just before he died. His name was Tracker; he was a German shorthair pointer: the same breed as Major. I had him for about two months and he was learning fast.

One afternoon I had Tracker out to work with me at the airplane hangar. I was busy cleaning up some parts when Tracker started scratching at the door. I was glad that he let me know that he needed to go outside 'to do his duty.' I opened the door and he ran right out.

I went back to cleaning parts. A couple minutes later, I opened the door to call Tracker back inside. There was blood everywhere. As I looked around, I noticed a couple of ladies standing nearby, and I also saw Tracker under my pickup truck.

The ladies asked me if that was my dog.

I said, "Yeah."

They told me that they had just hit him with their car on the nearby road.

I grimaced, because I knew this was not going to be good.

After some struggle, I got Tracker into the truck and took him to the veterinarian.

The vet looked him over and showed me that he had two legs that were ripped open to the bone. He had torn muscles and ligaments, broken bones, and messed up joints. There was no way that he could fix everything. He said that he would do what he could to keep him alive, but at best he would only ever have two good legs, and that was if he didn't get an infection, or other complications. It would take a couple months of recovery and several thousands of dollars in expenses.

After praying and giving it lots of thought, I decided to let him go back to God and I told the vet my decision.

The vet gave him a shot to put him to sleep. I petted Tracker as he slowly relaxed and fell into a deep sleep. Then the vet gave him the final shot.

My daughter, Kayla, showed up during this time to help comfort me.

It was a terrible thing to have to make this life-ending decision for the second time in just a couple of months.

Afterwards, I told Kayla that I was going to the airport to clean up the bloodstains that Tracker had left all around the hangar.

On the way I was praying to God, asking him, "Why did Tracker have to die?"

When I arrived at the airport I could see blood all around the door threshold, even up around the doorposts on each side.

It reminded me of the Passover described in Exodus 12 of The Bible, where the Israelites killed a lamb and spread its blood over the doorposts of the house so that the 'Angel of Death' would pass over the house and not kill the first born child of the family.

The Jews celebrate the Passover each year to remind them of when this happened to their ancestors, during the plagues that God sent against Egypt while the Israelites were enslaved there.

Then God reminded me of this verse from Isaiah, "Others died that you might live. I traded their lives for yours because you are precious to me. You are honored, and I love you" (Isaiah 43:4, NLT).

God showed me that Tracker died to remind me that *the wages of sin is death* (Romans 6:23), and that someone or something has to die to pay for the penalty of sin. His Son died for me so that I might live. He traded His life for mine because I am precious to Him and He loves me (and God loves you, too)!

God showed me that the reason this was happening, is because of the sin in my life that I was struggling with and having trouble overcoming (I had prayed to God to help me by changing my heart so that I would not even think of sinning against Him anymore).

At this time, I was also reminded of these verses from Isaiah 53. This was prophesied more than four hundred years before Christ came into the world.

> Who has believed our message? To whom has the LORD revealed his powerful arm? My servant grew up in the LORD's presence like a tender green shoot, like a root in dry ground. There was nothing beautiful or majestic about his appearance, nothing to attract us to him. He was despised and rejected— a man of sorrows, acquainted with deepest grief. We turned our backs on him and looked the other way. He was despised, and we did not care.

> Yet it was our weaknesses he carried; it was our sorrows that weighed him down. And we thought his troubles were a punishment from God, a punishment for his own sins! But he was pierced for our rebellion, crushed for our sins. He was beaten so we could be whole. He was whipped so we could be healed. All of us, like sheep, have strayed away. We have left God's paths to follow our own. Yet the LORD laid on him the sins of us all.

> He was oppressed and treated harshly, yet he never said a word. He was led like a lamb to the slaughter. And as a sheep is silent before the shearers, he did not open his mouth. Unjustly condemned, he was led away No one cared that

he died without descendants, that his life was cut short in midstream. But he was struck down for the rebellion of my people. He had done no wrong and had never deceived anyone. But he was buried like a criminal; he was put in a rich man's grave.

But it was the LORD's good plan to crush him and cause him grief. Yet when his life is made an offering for sin, he will have many descendants. He will enjoy a long life, and the LORD's good plan will prosper in his hands. When he sees all that is accomplished by his anguish, he will be satisfied. And because of his experience, my righteous servant will make it possible for many to be counted righteous, for he will bear all their sins. I will give him the honors of a victorious soldier, because he exposed himself to death. He was counted among the rebels. He bore the sins of many and interceded for rebels.

Isaiah 53:1–12 (NLT)

This all happened right before Christmas. You would think that this would have spoiled my Christmas... and in a way it did, but it also made quite an impact, reminding me that Christmas was about God's love sent down to us from heaven, in the form of the Christ-child.

"For God so loved the world that He gave His only begotten Son, that whoever believes in Him should not perish but have everlasting life" (John 3:16, NKJV).

So you see how God used scripture once again, to speak to me.

Other times God just speaks plainly to me, like a friend.

A while back I lost my checkbook. I looked everywhere that I could think of, but I couldn't find it.

After several days of looking, I finally went to God in prayer. As I prayed, God put this thought into my head, *Maybe I lost it while I was raking leaves.* So, I walked all over the yard looking and praying. I walked into the shed that I keep the lawnmower in (I had been using it to blow leaves off the yard and into the woods). There on the seat was my checkbook. It must have slid out of my pocket while I was mowing.

I was so happy that I had found it, and as I walked up toward the house, I was praising God for showing me where my checkbook was.

Then He said to me, "*But Ken, you never asked me where your watch is.*"

I exclaimed with a chuckle, "Okay, God, show me where my watch is!"

I hadn't seen my watch for three months. I kept thinking that I would find it sometime.

My wife even bought me a cheap replacement watch to use in the meantime, while I continued looking.

The next day God put the desire in my heart to clean up the boat and put it away for the winter. As I was vacuuming the deck and seats I happened to glance into the cup holder on the steering console and there was my watch!

Now you could say that this was just a coincidence, but I say that it was God who put those thoughts into my mind and directed me so that I could find these things that were lost.

A couple of weeks later I lost my watch again (if you can believe it)!

After looking for it for three days, I thought, *God showed me where my watch was last time; why wouldn't He show me again?*

So I sat on the edge of my bed and prayed, "Heavenly Father, you showed me where my watch was when I lost it before—I lost my watch again, could you please show me where it is once more?"

When I opened my eyes, I saw that my clothes hamper was overflowing with dirty clothes, so I took it to the laundry chute to empty it. I was grabbing handfuls of clothes, throwing them down the chute. As I went to grab the last handful, I looked into the hamper and there on top of the last bit of clothes was my watch!

I have no idea how it got there. It could have been anywhere. I could just have easily grabbed my watch along with my clothes and never even noticed. Yet there was my watch, lying there, like someone had just placed it in plain view.

Again you could say that this was just a coincidence. But how many coincidences can happen the same way before one realizes that they are not a coincidence?

I find that God always leaves an opening for us, to explain these leadings, signs, and miracles away as only coincidence (if that is what we desire), but I know without any doubt that this was from God!

Shortly after this happened, I was visiting my sister in the hospital. My mom was there too; she was telling us about losing the diamond from her ring that she had inherited from her dad. Mom and Dad looked all over the house, even in the traps of drains from the bathtub and sinks, but they could not find the diamond.

I asked Mom, "Why don't you pray to God and ask Him to show you where it is?" Then I told her about the story of how God showed me where my checkbook and watch were.

She and my sister listened to the story with open mouths and big eyes, and afterwards Mom asked, "Ken why don't you pray for God to show me where my diamond is?"

I just shook my head back and forth, and said, "No, Mom, you need to pray to God yourself."

My mom was missing the most important point—she was more interested in finding her stone than she was in having a personal relationship with God.

I wish she had asked me, "How can I have a personal relationship with God like you do?" Then I could have told her.

I share these experiences with you so that you will know that this kind of personal relationship with God is available, and not just to me, but to all people who seek God with all of their heart and soul. I have no special power in me, only the power of God, who lives in me. And He can, and will, live in you, too, if you ask Him into your heart, and into your life.

Seeking God

If you really want to know God, you need to earnestly seek Him!

"But if from there you seek the LORD your God, you will find him if you look for him with all your heart and with all your soul" (Deuteronomy 4:29, NIV).

When was the last time that you did something with all your heart and soul? Think about what you are most passionate about and how you pursue that interest... this is the way that God wants you to seek Him!

I am an avid hunter/fisherman. I love the outdoors. I love being out in God's creation, experiencing the beauty and wonder of all God has made, and I love the thrill of the hunt.

The first thing that a hunter needs to know to be successful is to learn all that he can about the game that he is hunting.

This can be accomplished by reading about what others have experienced, or through your own experiences. You need to know as much as you can about the game you pursue; for example what your game looks like, sounds like, and what kind of food it eats. You need to know its habits, where it feeds, where it sleeps, where it travels and when it does these things and why.

You need to use all of the senses that God has given you while you are hunting. You need to be looking and listening intently at all times, because you never know when or where you will find what you are seeking. It could show up at any time, even when you least expect it!

After you know as much as you can about the game that you seek, you must apply what you have learned. You must actually go hunting! It is the same way with knowing God. We can know everything there is to know about God, but still not know God. We must apply what we know to our life.

Much of what I have learned about hunting can also be used in seeking God. The best way to hunt for God is by reading The Bible. It is packed full of stories of how others came to know the LORD. Through these stories, we can come to know much about the character and ways of God. In fact, each character in The Bible can teach us something about our own character as well.

Whenever I sit down to read The Bible, the first thing I do is pray for the Holy Spirit to guide me into truth. I have been told so many false teachings about God, that knowing the truth about God was the thing that I desired more than anything, and this is the role of the Holy Spirit, "But you have received the Holy Spirit, and he lives within you, so you don't need anyone to teach you what is true. For the Spirit teaches you all things, and what he teaches is true—it is not a lie" (1 John 2:27, NLT).

While reading the Bible, I take notes. When I come across a verse that "jumps out at me," or makes some impression upon me, or that provides me with some insight about

God that I'm seeking at the time, I stop and pray about that verse. Then I meditate on the verse and ask God to reveal to me what it is that he wants me to know about this verse. Then I write the verse in my notebook under a topic that it fits under best. After a while I have many verses under several topics.

In my study time, I will choose a particular topic to study. I find that the verses I have collected each add a little information about the topic; or it is like adding a piece to a puzzle. We can't see the whole picture by just one piece of a puzzle, but when we put all of the pieces together we can, and this leads to, what I call, a "Spiritual Truth."

Another thing this method does for me is it gives me a wide variety of topics to teach from, and I already have several verses collected to back up my teachings. In fact I am using the verses that I have collected for each topic that I write about in this book.

The more that I read and study the Bible, the more that I realize how simple and basic God's truths really are, and this truth of seeking God is no exception.

It is as simple to understand as playing the game Hide-and-Seek when we were children. God is the one hiding and we are the one who is supposed to do the seeking, and if we don't seek, we don't find, period.

And this is the way that God likes it to be. Jesus prayed, "Oh Father, LORD of heaven and earth, thank you for hiding the truth from those who think themselves so wise and clever, and for revealing it to the childlike. Yes Father, it pleased you to do it this way" (Matthew 11:25–26, NLT)!

Let's take a look in the Bible at an example of the principle of seeking God, through the life of King Asa, found in 2 Chronicles, chapters 14–16. Please pause and read these chapters.

You will notice from chapter 14, "He commanded the people of Judah to seek the Lord, the God of their ancestors, and to obey his law and his commands. Asa also removed the pagan shrines, as well as the incense altars from every one of Judah's towns. So Asa's kingdom enjoyed a period of peace" (2 Chronicles 14:4, 5).

"All in Judah were happy about this covenant, for they had entered into it with all their heart. They earnestly sought after God, and they found him. And the Lord gave them rest from their enemies on every side" (2 Chronicles 15:15, NLT).

Whenever King Asa and the people under his reign sought the Lord, they found Him, and He gave them rest from their enemies. But in the later years of King Asa's life, he quit seeking God. "In the thirty-ninth year of his reign, Asa developed a serious foot disease. Yet even with the severity of his disease, he did not seek the Lord's help but turned only to his physicians. So he died in the forty-first year of his reign" (2 Chronicles 16:12–13, NLT).

King Asa would not seek the Lord to help with his foot disease, and because of it, he died from his condition.

I noticed from my own experiences that whenever I seek the Lord and walk alongside of Him, that God gives me rest from the struggles of life. But when I am walking in sin (and we all sin at one time or another) that sin brings many struggles with it. It is because God is just, and He disciplines us to keep us on the "path that leads to righteousness."

However, times of struggle in life are not always because of our own sin; sometimes we are the victims of someone else's sin, and sometimes struggles come to test our hearts or to build our character, to grow our perseverance, or increase our faith, or to get us to trust God and depend on Him more, to name a few.

The only way to know why we are facing a certain struggle is to seek the LORD, and He will reveal the answers to us, in His timing.

This verse in particular has an important message for us: "The LORD will stay with you as long as you stay with him! Whenever you seek him, you will find him. But if you abandon him, he will abandon you" (2 Chronicles 15:2, NLT).

Before leaving 2 Chronicles, please note that the LORD also seeks us: "The eyes of the LORD search the whole earth in order to strengthen those whose hearts are fully committed to him" (2 Chronicles 16:9, NLT).

This is also reiterated in the words that David spoke to Solomon while he was instructing him prior to his death: "And you, my son Solomon, acknowledge the God of your father, and serve him with wholehearted devotion and with a willing mind, for the LORD searches every heart and understands every motive behind the thoughts. If you seek him, he will be found by you, but if you forsake him, he will reject you forever" (1 Chronicles 28:9, NIV).

The Bible says, "Draw near to God and He will draw near to you" (James 4:8, NKJV).

Why should we spend time seeking God? Because, the Bible tells us that God rewards seekers, "And without faith it is impossible to please God, because anyone who comes to him must believe that he exists and that he rewards those who earnestly seek him (Hebrews 11:6, NIV).

And again, "The LORD is wonderfully good to those who wait for him and seek him" (Lamentations 3:25, NLT).

As an example of how God rewards those who seek Him, I'd like to share this story with you.

There was a knock at the door of my airplane hangar. It was "the friendly neighborhood tax assessor."

The first thing he did was start shooting a laser-measuring tool across the room, to find the width and length of my hangar.

I said to him, "It's 70x60 feet."

He confirmed, "Oh—yes it is." Then he told me, "I haven't been able to find your building on the tax records."

I replied, "Well, I've been paying property taxes since I built the hangar in 1997. I even have a recent tax assessment on my desk that came in the mail. I'll go get it."

I returned with the document and showed it to him. He looked like he was surprised that I was actually telling the truth.

He looked it over and stated, "This tax seems kind of high."

Now I was surprised to hear that coming from him. I replied, "Yeah, I pay more in taxes on my hangar than other people pay in rent for the city-owned hangars next door."

Then he surprised me even further when he came back with this statement, "I'll check this out against what the other hangar-owners are being charged for property tax and get back to you on what I find out.

I said, "Okay," while laughing under my breath, because I thought to myself, *Yeah sure you will!*

I figured I would never see him again.

But I was proven wrong once more when about a week later he came knocking at the door again.

He said, "I checked your tax against what the other hangar owners at the airport are paying, and you are paying twice as much as the others; so I cut your tax in half."

Now that made my jaw about drop to the floor. I thought, *This has to be a first; I have never heard of anyone's tax ever getting lowered like this!*

All I could say was, "Thanks."

He replied, "Yeah, sure. *It's all about Jesus* anyway. Right?"

Then it hit me what was happening; this was certainly God at work here. I thought, *This must be a reward from God for having the slogan, "It's all about JESUS" on the side of my hangar, because something like this just doesn't happen without God orchestrating it.*

I blurted out, "Yeah, it is!" And he left.

God really does reward those who seek Him and follow Him!

A couple of years before this, I was convicted by God of being a "closet" Christian (I was a Christian, but I didn't tell others about Him), until I read these words of Jesus, "If anyone acknowledges me publicly here on earth, I will openly acknowledge that person before my father in heaven. But if anyone denies me here on earth, I will deny that person before my father in heaven" (Matthew 10:32–33, NLT).

Then one day as I was driving up to the airport, I thought, *The side of my hangar would make a great billboard.*

At first I thought, *I could put up a billboard advertising my business.* But as I thought about it further, I decided I should put God first in my life and I said to myself, *I know, I'll put up a billboard for God.*

I started out putting "Wise Men Seek Him" on the side of my hangar during the Christmas season, keeping in line with the three wise men that sought out Jesus after he was born, by following the star that led them to him. I thought, *This saying is still true today.*

After a couple years of having this slogan up for Christmas I decided to change it to say, "It's all about JESUS" because that is what Christmas is all about.

Then on the second year, it was Easter season, and I still hadn't taken the sign down, but I thought, *Easter is all about Jesus, too.* Then after Easter, I thought, *All of life is really, all about Jesus.* So, now I leave it up all year, adding a star at Christmas time, and a cross for Easter season.

I used to think that the things God did for me and revealed to me were personal, and I didn't share them with anyone. I also thought that if I did share them with others, they would probably think that I'm crazy. But God showed me that we should share our experiences with others so that they too can get to know God better. Besides, we all have different experiences to share, and God wants it this way, so that none of us will become self-reliant. He wants us to relate with one another and to learn from each other's experiences. He made us to be relational, just as he wants a relationship with each of us.

Jesus tells us in the Book of Matthew, "But seek first the kingdom of God and His righteousness, and all these things shall be added to you" (Matthew 6:33, NKJV). In other words, if we make God our primary concern, God will look after our needs, and He already knows all of our needs!

This reminds me of a time when I went to buy an airplane for my business. The owner was the widow of a crop duster. As we pulled up to the hangar where the airplane was being serviced, she began to pour out her heart to me about all of the things that had happened in her life since the death of her husband. She told me how one of her sons had become bitter toward her and wanted his share of the inheritance immediately, and when he didn't get it, he had abandoned the family.

As we sat in the vehicle talking, the two mechanics were inside waiting for us to come in to examine the airplane. I was really crunched for time, but as I thought about this, I felt that God wanted me to sit and listen to this widow's story. So, I said a quick prayer to God, "If you will look after my business, I will look after yours," and I obeyed God by sitting with this widow listening to her, consoling her, and witnessing to her, and I trusted God to take care of the rest.

Eventually, I made it inside to check over the airplane and made a deal with this widow, and bought the airplane. But I was also able to witness to her and her new husband that evening about many of the things that God was doing in my life, and they also shared many things with me.

On another occasion, I was doing some work around the yard when all of a sudden God said to me, "Come to the mountain."

I stood there wondering what God meant, I responded, "What do you mean...what mountain?" (I'm a Minnesota flatlander. There are no mountains anywhere near me). I remember thinking, *does God want me to get in my pickup truck and drive to the mountains to meet Him there? And if so, which mountain? There are lots of mountains in the western states.*

I prayed about this, and thought about this for months, wondering what God meant by this. Then I made plans to go to the mountains while I was going to be in California for an "extreme" flight-training course that my friend, Kyle, and I were attending. We would be flying with a renowned aerobatic/spray-pilot Wayne Handley. He was going to show us how to recover from many kinds of unusual flight situations. This would be helpful in case we ever got ourselves into an unusual situation while spraying crops.

The course was a blast! It was very challenging and rewarding, and afterwards my wife and I headed to the mountains to meet with God. We were not on much of a mountain, but more like in the midst of the Redwood forests, but I took my Bible and went for a hike. I found a big tree to sit under, then I prayed, asking God to show me what He wanted to reveal to me.

As I sat there, God started to remind me of how Moses went to the top of Mt. Sinai to meet with Him, and to receive the Ten Commandments, and how God also met with Elijah on the top of the mountain to reveal Himself to him. I also remembered how Peter, James, and John witnessed Jesus as He was transfigured on a mountain, and how Moses and Elijah also appeared there, as God spoke from a cloud saying, "This is my Son, whom I love; with him I am well pleased. Listen to him!"(Matthew 17:5, NIV). I also remembered that Jesus often retreated to the mountains to escape the crowds when He wanted some quiet time to spend with God in prayer.

Then I finally realized what God was trying to tell me. By telling me to "come to the mountain," He was really saying that He wanted me to spend more time with Him, and the reason that He didn't make this more clear to me right away, was to get me to spend time seeking Him.

I now try to spend some time in devotion and prayer every day. Even during our busy work season, I do this, along with my family and/or employees. I feel it is so important to start the day by putting God first and foremost in our thoughts.

Some people think that they have all the time in the world to seek God, but this is not true. Our days on earth are numbered and none of us knows when our time is up. So, it's important to seek God while there is still time. Like God said through the prophet Isaiah, "Seek the LORD while you can find him. Call on him now while he is near" (Isaiah 55:6, NLT).

An example of this can be found in the story of the ten bridesmaids from Matthew 25:1–13 that I shared with you earlier. Five of them were ready for Christ's return, while five of them were not and were locked out of the Kingdom of God. They did not spend their time on earth wisely by getting to know Jesus while they were here.

I know of many people in America who have Bibles sitting in their homes, but seldom, if ever, read them. I always think, *What are they going to say when they stand before "the judgment seat of Christ" and Jesus asks them, "What do you mean 75 years (or however long they were on earth), was not enough time to read My Word."* The very dust on top of their Bible will convict them.

Another example of this importance of seeking God now, while there is still time, can be found in the story of The Rich Man and Lazarus told by Jesus:

> There was a rich man who was dressed in purple and fine linen and lived in luxury every day. At his gate was laid a beggar named Lazarus, covered with sores and longing to eat what fell from the rich man's table. Even the dogs came and licked his sores.
>
> The time came when the beggar died and the angels carried him to Abraham's side. The rich man also died and was buried. In hell, where he was in torment, he looked up and saw Abraham far away, with Lazarus by his side. So he called to him, "Father Abraham, have pity on me and send Lazarus to dip the tip of his finger in water and cool my tongue, because I am in agony in this fire."

> But Abraham replied, "Son, remember that in your lifetime you received your good things, while Lazarus received bad things, but now he is comforted here and you are in agony. And besides all this, between us and you a great chasm has been fixed, so that those who want to go from here to you cannot, nor can anyone cross over from there to us."
>
> He answered, "Then I beg you, father, send Lazarus to my father's house, for I have five brothers. Let him warn them, so that they will not also come to this place of torment."
>
> Abraham replied, "They have Moses and the Prophets; let them listen to them."
>
> "No, father Abraham," he said, "but if someone from the dead goes to them, they will repent."
>
> He said to him, "If they do not listen to Moses and the Prophets, they will not be convinced even if someone rises from the dead."
>
> Luke 16:19–31 (NIV)

We can read about the warnings of Moses and the Prophets, in The Bible, anytime that we want to; so none of us will be able to use the excuse, "But, I never knew!"

When I read this, it reminds me of my own siblings, as well as others, and I wonder which of them might know about God—but not know God personally. And I think of how I once was "dead in my own sins," but now am "alive in Christ." I feel that God brought me back from spiritual death and saved me, so that I could warn others of this impending doom, and tell them how to have eternal life by putting their faith in Jesus Christ.

But even more importantly, is the fact that we have a Savior who has risen from the dead, and his name is Jesus Christ. We just need to listen to Him and put our faith in Him.

Therefore, I urge you to seek the "God of the Bible," because the Holy Bible contains the words of God, and these words lead to eternal life. Have faith in God and believe in His son Jesus Christ. Follow Him and His ways; be obedient to what He calls you to do. To know what God has called you to do, you need to know God. And in order to know God, you need to seek Him with all of your heart and soul!

> "Keep on asking, and you will receive what you ask for. Keep on seeking, and you will find. Keep on knocking, and the door will be opened to you. For everyone who asks, receives. Everyone who seeks, finds. And to everyone who knocks, the door will be opened."
>
> Matthew 7:7–8, (NIV)

The Power of Prayer

So, what is prayer? Prayer is simply our way of communicating with God.

Jesus taught His disciples to pray like this:

> And when you pray, do not be like the hypocrites, for they love to pray standing in the synagogues and on the street corners to be seen by men. I tell you the truth, they have received their reward in full. But when you pray, go into your room, close the door and pray to your Father, who is unseen. Then your Father, who sees what is done in secret, will reward you. And when you pray, do not keep on babbling like pagans, for they think they will be heard because of their many words. Do not be like them, for your Father knows what you need before you ask him.

This, then, is how you should pray:

> "Our Father in heaven, hallowed be your name, your kingdom come, your will be done on earth as it is in heaven. Give us today our daily bread. Forgive us our debts, as we also have forgiven our debtors. And lead us not into temptation, but deliver us from the evil one."
>
> Matthew 6:5–13 (NIV)

This prayer is often referred to as the LORD's Prayer. But Jesus never intended this to be an exact prayer to be recited word for word; it is an outline of how we should pray. This is verified by the preceding verses that tell us not to babble by repeating the same words over and over.

Prayer is not something we do to impress others about how religious we are. It is not to be self-edifying.

It's intended to be done in humility, giving reverence to God, because God is sovereign and worthy of our respect.

Next, Jesus teaches us to pray expectantly for His Kingdom to be established on the earth (which will happen when He returns).

We are to pray for God's will to be done (this is so important, because often times God's will and God's ways are so much different than our own (but always better) (Isaiah 55:8–9). We must always remember that God is sovereign... He is LORD of everything! God's will must always come before our own.

Jesus prayed for God's will to be done when He prayed in the Garden of Gethsemane for this "cup of suffering" to pass Him by if possible (Matthew 26:39). Even though Jesus prayed profusely, He still desired the Father's will over His own, and we know that God did not allow this cup to pass Him by because it was the very reason that Jesus was sent into the world—to bear the penalty for our sins upon

Himself, by being beaten, mocked, whipped, and finally to die a criminal's death on the cross, and then to rise again three days later.

Next, we are to pray to receive the necessities of life. These are the things that we need, not necessarily the things we want. God is not our "genie-in-a-bottle" whose purpose is to make our every wish come true.

Finally, we all need our sins forgiven, because we all have sinned against someone at some time, and because Christ first forgave us, we also need to forgive others. "For if you forgive men when they sin against you, your heavenly Father will also forgive you. But if you do not forgive men their sins, your Father will not forgive your sins" (Matthew 6:14–15, NIV). We cannot hold a grudge against another, and expect God to answer our prayers. We need to make things right with that person. We need to forgive others, just as Christ first forgave us.

We need to pray for God's strength to help us overcome the temptations and schemes of Satan because spiritual warfare is real! Satan is at war with God's children.

Prayer is at the very heart of how we have a personal relationship with God. Even though God already knows our needs, he still loves to hear from us. We simply talk to him like a child would talk to his father.

An element of prayer that is often overlooked is the importance of listening. Sometimes we don't get an answer to prayer because we fail to take the time to listen. Communication can't be one-way; it takes both talking and listening.

Another important thing to remember about prayer is that the gifts (or things we pray for) should never be desired more than the giver. As a father myself, I love to give my children good gifts, but I don't appreciate it when my children want only what I can give them, but don't want to have a relationship with me.

It's like being invited to someone's house for dinner and not speaking to your host, but only grabbing what food they have to offer, and then leaving.

Unfortunately, we have all prayed at times when God didn't give us what we asked for, or God answered our prayers differently than we would have liked.

So, let's look at some of the possible reasons for this:

James tells us, "You do not have, because you do not ask God. When you ask, you do not receive, because you ask with wrong motives, that you may spend what you get on your own personal pleasures" (James 4:2b-3, NLT).

How many times do we plunge into something without praying first, and then wonder what went wrong when things don't work out?

At other times it may be because we are praying with selfish motives, or wrong motives, such as to use the gifts of God for our own glory.

At other times, it is because of our lack of faith- "But when he asks, he must believe and not doubt, because he who doubts is like a wave of the sea, blown and tossed by the wind. That man should not think he will receive anything from the LORD" (James 1:6–7, NIV).

Paul tells us to "Pray at all times and on every occasion in the power of the Holy Spirit. Stay alert and be persistent in your prayers for all Christians everywhere" (Ephesians 6:18, NLT).

We should pray for the needs of others as well as for our own needs.

This verse, as well as the following parable, reminds us to be persistent in our prayers—never giving up!

> Then, teaching them more about prayer, Jesus used this story: "Suppose you went to a friend's house at midnight, wanting to borrow three loaves of bread. You say to him, 'A friend of mine has just arrived for a visit, and I have nothing for him to eat.' And suppose he calls out from his bedroom, 'Don't bother me. The door is locked for the night, and my family and I are all in bed. I can't help you.' But I tell you this—though he won't do it for friendship's sake, if you keep knocking long enough, he will get up and give you whatever you need because of your shameless persistence.
>
> And so I tell you, keep on asking, and you will receive what you ask for."
>
> Luke 11:5–9a (NLT)

Sometimes God answers our prayers immediately! Other times we need to pray persistently for a very long time before God answers us.

Another thing that Jesus teaches us about prayer is to pray in His name. Why do we ask in Jesus' name? Because it's through His sacrifice (when He died on the cross), that opened the way for us to go directly to the Father in prayer.

> Now the first covenant had regulations for worship and also an earthly sanctuary. A tabernacle was set up. In its first room were the lampstand, the table, and the consecrated bread; this was called the Holy Place. Behind the second curtain was a room called the Most Holy Place, which had the golden altar of incense and the gold-covered

ark of the covenant. This ark contained the gold jar of manna, Aaron's staff that had budded, and the stone tablets of the covenant. Above the ark were the cherubim of the Glory, overshadowing the atonement cover. But we cannot discuss these things in detail now.

When everything had been arranged like this, the priests entered regularly into the outer room to carry on their ministry. But only the high priest entered the inner room, and that only once a year, and never without blood, which he offered for himself and for the sins the people had committed in ignorance. The Holy Spirit was showing by this that the way into the Most Holy Place had not yet been disclosed as long as the first tabernacle was still standing.

Hebrews 9:1–8 (NIV)

During the old system of animal sacrifice for the sins of the people, only the High Priest could go before God, into the Most Holy Place, and only once a year. But when Jesus died on the cross, the curtain that separated God from man was torn in two from top to bottom, opening up God to all people.

"And when Jesus had cried out again in a loud voice, he gave up his spirit. At that moment the curtain of the temple was torn in two from top to bottom. The earth shook and the rocks split" (Matthew 27:50–51, NIV).

"And so, dear friends, we can boldly enter heaven's Most Holy Place because of the blood of Jesus. This is the new, life-giving way that Christ has opened up for us through the sacred curtain, by means of his death for us" (Hebrews 10:19–20, NLT).

What a privilege it is to be able to boldly enter the sanctuary of God, right before His throne, and ask God for anything that we need. And it is by Jesus' sacrifice that we are able to do this, and that is why we ask in His holy name, because without His blood covering our sins, we would not be able to do this.

> Jesus said, "I tell you the truth, anyone who believes in me will do the same works I have done, and even greater works, because I am going to be with the Father. You can ask for anything in my name, and I will do it, so that the Son can bring glory to the Father. Yes, ask me for anything in my name, and I will do it!"
>
> John 14:12–14 (NLT)

Here Jesus tells us that anyone who believes in Him will do the same works that He has done and even greater works.

Have you read about all the miracles and great works that Jesus did while He walked the earth? Yet here Jesus is telling us that we can do the same, or even more.

"But if you remain in me and my words remain in you, you may ask for anything you want, and it will be granted" (John 15:7, NLT).

So does this really mean that God will give us anything that we ask for? The Bible tells us that He will, but it needs to be in line with His will, for the right motives, and for His purposes and His glory. We also must stay connected to Him—especially if we are to know His will.

A few verses later, Jesus says it like this: "You didn't choose me. I chose you. I appointed you to go and produce lasting fruit, so that the Father will give you whatever you ask for, using my name" (John 15:16, NLT).

I believe God calls all Christians to bear fruit. Just like an apple tree has not become all that God created it to be until it produces fruit, so we who are Christians haven't become all that God has created us to be, until we too bear fruit. Though we are all called to produce fruit, only a few ever accept the call.

"For many are called, but few are chosen" (Matthew 22:14, NKJV).

When we use the spiritual gifts that God gives us and we use the things that we ask for to produce fruit (to bring others into the Kingdom of God), this pleases God very much; because this brings glory to God, and this is what God has called us to do. This is being right in the middle of God's will as His disciples.

There are many ways to produce fruit; sometimes we plant seeds, sometimes we water and nurture, while other times we harvest. All are important steps in bringing others to faith.

> At that time you won't need to ask me for anything. I tell you the truth, you can ask the Father directly, and he will grant your request because you use my name. You haven't done this before. Ask, using my name, and you will receive, and you will have abundant joy.
>
> John 16:23–24 (NLT)

Some religions still teach that we need to pray through a priest, or through people that have died before us, or through Mary (the mother of Jesus), the saints, or whatever other intercessory that people can imagine, but the truth is, we can and should, go directly to the Father in prayer.

Jesus continues, "Then you will ask in my name. I'm not saying I will ask the Father on your behalf, for the Father himself loves you dearly because you love me and believe that I came from God" (John 16:26–27, NLT).

In fact Jesus tells us that we don't even have to pray through Him. We can ask the Father directly (in the name of Jesus), for God loves us dearly because of our faith in Christ.

I've found that whenever Jesus repeats Himself, the reader had better be paying attention, because He is telling us something extremely important. Here in the gospel of John, Jesus tells us that we can ask anything in His name, and God will give it to us, not just two times, but twice in each chapter, for three consecutive chapters, for a total of six times! Do you think this might be important? Indeed it is!

I noticed that in the midst of these scriptures, Jesus is talking about the importance of His disciples "bearing fruit." "My true disciples produce much fruit. This brings great glory to my Father" (John 15:8, NLT).

From my own experiences, I've found that when I ask God for something to use as a witness of Him and to bring glory to Him, that this is being right in the middle of God's will, and that He will give me whatever I ask for in Jesus' name at these times. Here are a couple examples of this:

It was the last night of the deer-hunting season, I opened my eyes after saying a prayer, and deer came running at me from every direction.

I was hunting with my brother, Ben, and his friends near

my hometown of Danube, Minnesota. It was the second consecutive year that I was able to hunt with them.

After becoming a Christian a few years earlier, I always look for opportunities to witness to family and friends about God. I thought that going deer hunting with them would possibly give me this opportunity.

The year before when I hunted with this group I shot three bucks and Ben and his friends just thought that I was lucky. One of them even asked me, "Why do you get to shoot all the deer?"

I told them, "It's because of my walk with God. He blesses me for following Him and His ways."

They just said, "Yeah, whatever!"

With two nights left of the deer-hunting season, Ben and I were hunting in a field near the Minnesota River, I saw a really nice buck, but it didn't come close enough for me to get a shot at it. I decided the next night to go back to that same area. I thought that the buck might return to the same place; only this time I would sit in a spot that was closer to where he appeared.

This was the last night of the season and we only had a couple of small deer so far. Ben didn't want to go back to the same place again; so another guy from our hunting party, Richard, went with me.

We got to the field a couple of hours before sunset. This is my favorite time to hunt, because the deer are most active right before the sun goes down. I put Richard in the exact spot that I saw the big buck the night before, hoping that he would have a good chance at seeing him. I went a couple hundred yards to the east. There was a climbable tree on the line fence, which divides Ben's field from his neighbors. I climbed the tree, got somewhat comfortable by standing on a branch and leaning against the trunk of the tree; then I closed my eyes to pray.

I prayed, "Dear Heavenly Father, could you please send me some deer so that I can use this to witness to my brother and his friends about you. I ask this in the name of Jesus, Amen."

I opened my eyes and immediately a small yearling deer came running toward my tree from out of the woods in front of me. Close behind was a doe. We had a couple of doe permits to fill in our party, but I only had a permit to shoot a buck. I usually let others fill their own doe tags, but I thought I would take a shot at this doe because she was pretty big. She was running so fast that I couldn't swing my gun through all the branches, fast enough to keep up with her, and I missed.

I looked up, and over the hill came an eight-point buck. It too was coming right toward my tree. I took aim and shot. The buck kept on running. I thought, *How could I have missed?* I shot again, and this time I could see blood squirting out both sides of the deer with each beat of its heart. I knew that I had made a fatal shot this time. The deer took a few more steps and then collapsed.

I looked up again, and a six-point buck came over the hill from the same direction, running right at my tree. It stopped broadside to me and just stood there. I lifted my gun again, took aim and shot. The deer dropped to his knees. I reached into my pocket for more ammunition. I loaded my gun while I watched the buck to see what he would do. I also looked around to see if God was going to send me any more deer. Whew! I took a deep breath; this was all happening so fast. No other deer came, so I took careful aim at the buck again (because it seemed like he was not going to die, and he was not going to run), I squeezed the trigger and toppled him with one more shot.

I looked over toward Richard; he was standing there staring at me with his mouth wide-opened. I yelled over at him, "We're done! Come on over."

As I was climbing down the tree, I spotted another fawn standing behind me.

Richard approached my tree just as I was getting back down to earth. He was chuckling now as he asked, "What are you doing?"

I answered, "I got two bucks down. Would you like to shoot a fawn?" I asked, as I pointed out the deer to him.

He was just shaking his head in wonderment. He said, "No, it's kind of small. Let it grow up a little."

Then I told him what happened.

It was absolutely amazing the way God answered my prayer so quickly. There is no other explanation except that God sent these deer to me.

I believe that God answered this prayer because I asked with right motives, and by that I mean, not for personal gain and glory, but for the glory of God. I didn't ask so that I could brag about what a good hunter I am; I asked so that I could use it as a witness to others about God.

The following winter, I was given another opportunity to witness about God sending the deer.

Ben called me on the phone and asked me to go ice fishing with him on Leech Lake. On the way there, I thought about how God had answered my prayer request to send deer, and I prayed again, this time for God to send us fish.

Ben and his friend, Kevin, own a house together, on Leech Lake. They hardly ever catch fish on this lake, though they have been fishing there for several years. They even refer to the lake as "The Dead Sea."

Ben and I went to a spot on the lake that he fishes regularly, though without much success. We drilled several holes through the ice at varying depths, ranging from seven to thirty feet. Then we tried the different depths to see where the fish were biting the best. I tried a couple holes with little success; then at about the ten foot depth, I started to get so many bites, that I couldn't keep the fish off my hook. I wasn't even putting bait on half the time. I yelled over to Ben to come over and look, but he was busy trying some of the other holes.

After I had about twenty-five fish lying on the ice, I yelled again for him to come look at the fish.

Finally he came over. He was surprised, and right away he said, "Let's set up the fish house here."

So we moved the house over the spot, drilled some more holes and continued fishing. I looked down the hole; I could see probably twenty fish just in one hole. We were catching fish as fast as we could get our hook back in the water. They weren't all keepers but we saved a five-gallon pail full!

The next morning we went back and caught another half pail of fish.

Ben and Kevin both commented that they never catch fish on this lake and asked, "Why do we catch fish when you're here?"

I told them that it was answer to prayer, that I had prayed all the way here that God would send us fish. I also reminded them of the time God had answered my prayer to send deer.

I know that these answers to prayer have made them think about what God did, and they have become more open to talking about God with me because of what they have witnessed.

I also used this miracle to witness to a young girl, who

I'll call Amy. She used to come to our church youth group, where I am a youth leader. I called her the following week to see how she was doing (because I found out from her dad that she had been in trouble with the law and was in lock-up for about eight months, but was now out on parole and doing much better).

I knew her from two years earlier, but I had lost touch with her when she quit coming to youth group. Now I was trying to reconnect with her in hopes of bringing her into a personal relationship with God.

While talking to her on the phone, we got to talking about fishing, and I told her about the great fishing that I had gotten into the week before. During that conversation, I mentioned that I could take her fishing sometime if she would like.

She called me twice the following week to see if Saturday would work out to take her fishing. I thought that since she had called me twice, she must really want to go, or this was from God, so I said I would.

We got to Leech Lake, set up the house in the same spot as the week before, put in our lines and waited for fish to bite. Nothing was happening.

I thought about how a couple weeks earlier I couldn't keep the fish off of my line; I also remembered that I had prayed for God to send us fish. With this thought fresh in my mind, I turned to Amy and asked her, "Will you pray with me for God to send us fish?"

She gave me an "are you crazy" kind of look, and said, "No-o-o!"

I replied, "Okay. But I'm going to pray that God will send me fish," and I bowed my head and prayed right there.

Immediately, I started to catch fish. They were small, but they were still fish. After catching several fish and Amy catching nothing, I told her to try my pole so she could catch fish. We switched poles, and again I was catching fish with Amy's pole and she was not even getting a nibble on mine.

I tried another hole in the ice, and I was still catching fish.

I went back to Amy's original hole, and still, I was catching fish while Amy caught nothing.

I said to Amy again, "Here, take your pole back, so you can catch some fish."

I traded poles and holes with Amy again, but no matter what we did, I caught fish, while Amy could not even get a bite.

The fish I was catching were getting bigger and bigger, and Amy's eyes were getting bigger and bigger!

Finally I asked Amy, "Are you ready to pray for God to send you fish?"

She looked down, and again she said, "No."

I continued to catch fish, while Amy caught nothing.

I told her how God sent me fish two weeks ago when I prayed, and I told her the story of how God sent me deer when I prayed, and I explained how I had become a believer in "asking God for anything in His name, and He will do it."

But she just quit fishing, while I continued to catch fish.

Finally she said, "I'm bored, I want to go home."

I said, "Okay," and we packed up and went home.

Amy never did humble herself and put her faith in God, even though she saw what God did, right before her very eyes, but I know that she has to be thinking about it.

A couple of Bible stories come to my mind as I think about what God did.

The first is from Luke chapter 5, when Jesus told Peter to cast out his nets, and he would catch many fish.

Peter replied that they had been fishing all night and caught nothing, but said they would try again.

This time they caught so many fish that their nets were tearing, and they filled two boats with fish. At this Peter, James, and John recognized the "power of God" and all of them decided right there, that they would drop everything and follow Jesus.

Jesus said to them, "Don't be afraid! From now on you will be fishing for men."

As disciples of Jesus, we too are called to be "Fishers of Men."

Then in John 21, Jesus appears to his disciples after His resurrection and He called to them from the shore, "Cast your nets on the other side of the boat and you will catch plenty of fish."

Again their nets were so full that they could not bring them in.

Jesus still does miracles like this today, to reveal Himself and His power, so that He can draw people to Himself.

I also thought about how Amy would not humble herself and pray even when she witnesses the power of God right before her very eyes! All of us need to do this; like the Scriptures say, "Then if My people who are called by My name will humble themselves, and pray and seek My face, and turn from their wicked ways, then I will hear from heaven, and will forgive their sin and heal their land" (2 Chronicles 7:14, NKJV).

It also reminded me that it is a personal choice, whether we will put our trust in God and follow Him. Nobody can do it for us, and this cannot be done corporately. It is not about belonging to the right church or religion, and nobody can make us believe. God has given us all free will, to choose for ourselves if we will follow Him.

"But if you are unwilling to serve the LORD, then choose

today whom you shall serve … but as for me and my household, we shall serve the Lord" (Joshua 24:15, NLT).

God's Call to Persevere

Salvation is not an end, but a beginning. It's not like a graduation—it's more like a wedding day, the start of a new relationship, when two people give their lives to each other. Jesus has already given His life for us; the least we can do is to give our life back to Him.

Whoever heard of a couple that gets married, and then goes their own separate way?

No, in a marriage, the two become one; they are joined to each other, just as we are now joined to Christ.

> I am the true grapevine, and my Father is the gardener. He cuts off every branch of mine that doesn't produce fruit, and he prunes the branches that do bear fruit so they will produce even more. You have already been pruned and purified by the message I have given you. Remain in me, and I will remain in you. For a branch cannot produce fruit if it is severed from the vine, and you cannot be fruitful unless you remain in me.

> Remain in me, and I will remain in you. For a branch cannot produce fruit if it is severed from the vine, and you cannot be fruitful unless you remain in me.
>
> Yes, I am the vine; you are the branches. Those who remain in me, and I in them, will produce much fruit. For apart from me you can do nothing. Anyone who does not remain in me is thrown away like a useless branch and withers. Such branches are gathered into a pile to be burned."
>
> John 15:1–6 (NLT)

These verses show the importance of staying close to God. Man can do nothing alone, and God could do everything without us, but praise God that He is a relational God, and He chooses to do His work through us. This way we can have an intimate and personal relationship with Him.

But if we choose to part from Jesus, going our own way, and doing our own thing, we will become useless to God for the advancement of His Kingdom in the world. We will become like dried up branches that wither and eventually die, and then are thrown into the fire.

We will become like the fig tree in this parable:

> Then he told this parable: "A man had a fig tree, planted in his vineyard, and he went to look for fruit on it, but did not find any. So he said to the man who took care of the vineyard, 'For three years now I've been coming to look for fruit on this fig tree and haven't found any. Cut it down! Why should it use up the soil?'

> 'Sir,' the man replied, 'leave it alone for one more year, and I'll dig around it and fertilize it. If it bears fruit next year, fine! If not, then cut it down.'"
>
> Luke 13:6–9 (NIV)

I know that some Christians believe that once you are saved—you are always saved. Some say that you cannot lose your salvation.

I believe that, though it is not probable, it is possible.

It's not probable, because of the Holy Spirit's presence in us, and His influence over us when we become a Christian.

But it is possible, because God never takes away our "free will." We always have the choice to reject Christ, even after becoming a Christian. That's why I say, "Salvation is about a daily decision to follow Christ."

The reason God doesn't take away our free will is because, as I found out through life's experiences, you cannot force someone to love you, or to forgive you, and you can't make someone believe. You can love another person with all of your heart, but you can't make them love you back; it is a choice that they must make, you can't make it for them. You can ask someone for forgiveness, but you can't make that person forgive you. It becomes their choice. And you can tell others about God, but you can't make them believe.

God knows that without free will, these things would not exist... they would not even be necessary. God would just control us like robots or puppets on a string.

Thank God that He is not like that. He desires a love relationship with each one of us. And all that He asks in return is that we believe in Him, to love Him with all of our hearts, and to love one another.

I believe that the only way we can lose our salvation is by

first coming to a full knowledge of the truth, and then rejecting it completely. This is what the scriptures mean when it says in three of the four gospels, "Sins against the Son of God can be forgiven, but blasphemy against the Holy Spirit will not be forgiven; in this life, or the next" (Mark 3:28–29, Luke 12:10, Matthew 12:31–32).

What I mean by coming to a full knowledge of the truth is knowing the gospel message, believing it, accepting it, and then rejecting it.

The reason that it's called blasphemy against the Holy Spirit is because it's the Holy Spirit that testifies to us about Jesus Christ, and it's the Holy Spirit that identifies us as His own on the day of our salvation (Eph. 4:30).

> For it is impossible to bring back to repentance those who were once enlightened—those who have experienced the good things of heaven and shared in the Holy Spirit, who have tasted the goodness of the Word of God and the power of the age to come—and who then turn away from God. It is impossible to bring such people back to repentance; by rejecting the Son of God, they themselves are nailing him to the cross once again and holding him up to public shame.
>
> Hebrews 6:4–6 (NLT)

> Dear friends, if we deliberately continue sinning after we have received knowledge of the truth, there is no longer any sacrifice that will cover these sins. There is only the terrible expectation of God's judgment and the raging fire that will consume his enemies. For anyone who refused

> to obey the law of Moses was put to death without mercy on the testimony of two or three witnesses. Just think how much worse the punishment will be for those who have trampled on the Son of God, and have treated the blood of the covenant, which made us holy, as if it were common and unholy, and have insulted and enraged the Holy Spirit who brings God's mercy to us.
>
> Hebrews 10:26–29 (NLT)

If God's way of making us right with Him is rejected, there is no other plan for the salvation of men in which we can pursue. There is only one way to God, and it is through His Son, Jesus Christ.

"Salvation is found in no one else, for there is no other name under heaven given to men by which we must be saved" (Acts 4:12, NIV).

Jesus answered, "I am the Way, the Truth and the Life. No one comes to the Father except through me" (John 14:6, NIV).

God clearly tells us how he will judge men who turn away.

"However; if righteous people turn to sinful ways and start acting like other sinners, should they be allowed to live? No, of course not! All their previous goodness will be forgotten, and they will die for their sins" (Ezekiel 18:24, NLT).

> And when people escape from the wicked ways of the world by learning about our LORD and Savior Jesus Christ and then get tangled up with sin and become its slave again, they are worse off than before. It would be better if they had never known the right way to live than to know it and then reject the holy commandments that

> were given to them. They make these proverbs come true: "A dog returns to its vomit," and "a washed pig returns to the mud."
>
> 2 Peter 2:20–22 (NLT)

And remember what Jesus said to the church of Sardis, "He who overcomes shall be clothed in white garments, and I will not blot out his name from the Book of Life; but I will confess his name before My Father and before His angels" (Revelation 3:5, NKJV).

Jesus would not have mentioned this, if erasing their names from the Book of Life were not possible.

So find out what pleases the LORD. Obey everything that He calls on you to do, and try to live a life that is worthy of being called "a child of God."

It's imperative to count the cost of being a disciple of Christ before starting down this road, because it is not an easy walk. This is what Jesus said to those following Him, about the cost of being His disciples.

> If anyone comes to me and does not hate his father and mother, his wife and children, his brothers and sisters—yes, even his own life—he cannot be my disciple. And anyone who does not carry his cross and follow me cannot be my disciple.
>
> Suppose one of you wants to build a tower. Will he not first sit down and estimate the cost to see if he has enough money to complete it? For if he lays the foundation and is not able to finish it, everyone who sees it will ridicule him, saying,

"This fellow began to build and was not able to finish."

Or suppose a king is about to go to war against another king. Will he not first sit down and consider whether he is able with ten thousand men to oppose the one coming against him with twenty thousand? If he is not able, he will send a delegation while the other is still a long way off and will ask for terms of peace. In the same way, any of you who does not give up everything he has cannot be my disciple.

Salt is good, but if it loses its saltiness, how can it be made salty again? It is fit neither for the soil nor for the manure pile; it is thrown out.

Luke 14:26–34 (NIV)

I urge you to persevere in your faith; for it comes with much persecution, trials, and strife.

But, it also comes with great rewards: "Consider it pure joy, my brothers, whenever you face trials of many kinds, because you know that the testing of your faith develops perseverance. Perseverance must finish its work so that you may be mature and complete, not lacking anything" (James 1:2–4, NIV).

"Blessed is the man who perseveres under trial, because when he has stood the test, he will receive the crown of life that God has promised to those who love him" (James 1:12, NIV).

Peter also confirms this:

> All praise to God, the Father of our Lord Jesus Christ. It is by his great mercy that we

have been born again, because God raised Jesus Christ from the dead. Now we live with great expectation, and we have a priceless inheritance—an inheritance that is kept in heaven for you, pure and undefiled, beyond the reach of change and decay. And through your faith, God is protecting you by his power until you receive this salvation, which is ready to be revealed on the last day for all to see.

So be truly glad. There is wonderful joy ahead, even though you have to endure many trials for a little while. These trials will show that your faith is genuine. It is being tested as fire tests and purifies gold—though your faith is far more precious than mere gold. So when your faith remains strong through many trials, it will bring you much praise and glory and honor on the day when Jesus Christ is revealed to the whole world.

You love him even though you have never seen him. Though you do not see him now, you trust him, and you rejoice with a glorious, inexpressible joy. The reward for trusting him will be the salvation of your souls.

1 Peter 1:3–9 (NLT)

In order to persevere in our faith, we must learn to rely, not on our own strength, but on God's strength, "For I can do all things through Christ, who gives me the strength I need"

(Philippians 4:13, NLT). We must strive to become all that God has created us to be, keeping our eyes focused on heaven.

I am not saying that if we sin after becoming a Christian, we will lose our salvation, (because none of us is perfect). But we should be striving to become more Christ-like in all that we say and do. We are all a work-in-progress.

> I don't mean to say that I have already achieved these things or that I have already reached perfection. But I press on to possess that perfection for which Christ Jesus first possessed me. No, dear brothers and sisters, I have not achieved it, but I focus on this one thing: Forgetting the past and looking forward to what lies ahead, I press on to reach the end of the race and receive the heavenly prize for which God, through Christ Jesus, is calling us.
>
> Philippians 3:12–14 (NLT)

And what is the prize?

"That is what the Scriptures mean when they say,

'No eye has seen, no ear has heard, and no mind has imagined what God has prepared for those who love him.'" (1 Corinthians 2:9, NLT).

"See I am coming soon, and my reward is with me, to repay all according to their deeds" (Revelation 22:12, NLT).

So, once again I want to stress the importance of a daily walk with God. The need to be in His Word, to bring everything to God in prayer, and to look for those times when God is calling you to join Him in His work of redemption.

Put your faith in God. Obey God. Get to know God as you seek Him with all of your heart and soul; then anything you ask for in prayer, in Jesus' name, God will give you, if it is in line with His will; and hold fast to your faith.

May God bless you, encourage you, and strengthen you, in your walk with Him!

Bibliography

Henry T. Blackaby and Claude V. King, *Experiencing God, Knowing and Doing the Will of God*, Copyright 1990, LifeWay Press, Nashville, Tennessee, Fifteenth Printing, May 1999, Unit 2, page 27.

Shout to the LORD, written and sang by Darlene Zschech, published by Hillsong Australia, Sydney, Australia, 1993.

Indiana Jones and the Last Crusade, 1989, directed by Steven Spielberg, produced by Robert Watts, Frank Marshall and Kathleen Kennedy, written by Jeffrey Boam and Tom Stoppard, story by George Lucas and Menno Meyjes, starring Harrison Ford as Indiana Jones.

e|LIVE

listen|imagine|view|experience

AUDIO BOOK DOWNLOAD INCLUDED WITH THIS BOOK!

In your hands you hold a complete digital entertainment package. Besides purchasing the paper version of this book, this book includes a free download of the audio version of this book. Simply use the code listed below when visiting our website. Once downloaded to your computer, you can listen to the book through your computer's speakers, burn it to an audio CD or save the file to your portable music device (such as Apple's popular iPod) and listen on the go!

How to get your free audio book digital download:

1. Visit www.tatepublishing.com and click on the e|LIVE logo on the home page.
2. Enter the following coupon code:
   8d3f-f026-4fd9-d648-62cd-8ea6-b8c3-c79f
3. Download the audio book from your e|LIVE digital locker and begin enjoying your new digital entertainment package today!